A WRETCH LII
A True Stor

To Mum
The strongest and most generous person I ever knew.
Miss you

1943 – 2017

To/ Rachel,

2 Corinthians 5:9,

Be encouraged & keep up the
"Good work" Mary.

IT'S NEVER TOO LATE.

A WRETCH LIKE ME
A True Story

Contact Martin Berry at: martinberry.ksm@gmail.com

ISBN 978-0-244-04459-6

MARTIN BERRY
Founder & Pastor of Legacy Church London
& Manifest Ministry International

A WRETCH **LIKE ME**
A True Story

IT'S NEVER TOO LATE.

COMMENDATIONS

Martin Berry is a personal friend, a friend of my family and the Church fellowship. It's a privilege therefore to be asked to present a few paragraphs about the man and his story. When reading this book you will be hooked, his story is compelling, surely God was up to something and He is still up to something in Martin's life.

I believe God set us up to meet, which is a story in itself. You wouldn't believe it but we met in Ikea and what attracted me to him was the rawness of his belief in Jesus Christ, which brought tears to my eyes as I sat in Ikea listening to him. There are no frills and the way he interprets the Bible is very interesting indeed. Since our meeting Martin has been to Eden to teach and preach and everyone loves him. I distinctly remember his teaching on 'Identity', which made an impact on everyone.

A scripture in the bible that came to mind immediately is found in Proverbs 3:6 *"In all thy ways acknowledge him, and he shall direct thy paths."* This verse was written in the opening pages of my first King James Bible at the age of 9. I understood this verse but as for the rest of the bible I did not have a clue what I was reading. Years later what I realised though, is that this verse really works when applied, and throughout the time I have known Martin he has applied this verse of the Bible to his life and in applying, he has experienced some interesting things, which has helped in the writing of this book. His story will change your life!

BRYON JONES, Senior Pastor, Eden Christian Centre,
The Apostolic Church UK, Ilford, London.

It is a great blessing knowing Martin Berry. I met him while on mission in England and his book; "A Wretch Like Me" has Salt. I'd compare it to Nicky Cruz' "Run Baby Run." This book will inspire and bless you, as it has me, and so many others in the United States.

CHARLIE MARTINEZ, Director, CM Ministries,
Houston, Texas, USA.

There is no other way to describe this book other than "wow!" Very few books have been forged through with blood, sweat and tears than this very powerful and intriguing book, it has been written with a sense of hope and faith of transformation to the reader. This unbelievable book is truly a gift to all who will embark on the journey of Pastor Martin Berry's life.

I thank God for placing the desire to write this book into the heart of Pastor Martin Berry, it is transformational, encouraging and full of insight. You will come to realize that even in someone else's setbacks and obstacles you too can overcome what life throws at you. I am grateful for our friendship and purpose filled relationship, every time we get together my life is expanded, energized, and encouraged.

I would encourage anyone who is interested in this book and the author to allow the Spirit of the Lord to lead you into this wonderful journey of purpose and prophetic insight on how God can restore, rebuild & reposition you for destiny.

MARTY PEREZ, Senior Pastor, House of Manna Church,
San Antonio, Texas, USA.

This the story of a man who, like the disciple Peter, is never stationary, waiting to see what will happen in life, but always jumping with both feet into new adventures with God. Through knowing him, my own faith has been stretched and sharpened, and I pray that as you read this book, you will find the same thing happening to you.

TIM WRAIGHT, Pastor, Legacy Church,
London, UK.

The bible says that every tree is know by his own fruit, meaning that if we know the fruit of someone we won't be wrong about them. I've known Pastor Martin since 2011 and I can say that he has a heart for God. I've seen his fruit in his lovely family, in his brave ministry and in his strong church. I am sure this book about such a fruitful man will impact the lives of many.

VINICIUS FERNANDES, Senior Pastor, Diversity Church,
London, UK.

I grew up in Tottenham just yards from Martin and knew him as one of the wild guys on our estate. While reading this superbly written book, I began to relive some of the heartbreak and horror that was so prevalent growing up in our neighbourhood. His story is living proof that God can reach into the worst hearts and transform lives from the inside out. His story is gripping, and the book takes hold of you and won't let you go until it's fully told.

I received a new sense of mission to reach out to those we think are 'impossible' to save as if any such person exists! I only found out in 2017 that Martin had committed living for God. By this time, he was a church planting leader, evangelist and successful mentor. This in itself is impressive bearing in mind that the last time I heard about him in my teenage years was when he was hanging upside down in a tree after a glue-sniffing episode!

I am sure you'll enjoy Martin's ministry, his anointing and his ability to reach out and hit you with the powerful, life-changing gospel.

PAUL NAUGHTON, Senior Pastor, Harvest Church,
London, UK.

I give continual thanks to God for Martin Berry for His perfect design and bringing our lives together at the right time, re-directing and transforming my life.

I am also truly and eternally grateful to Martin for his firm resolve and unwavering obedience to our Lord, and for his willingness to say what needs to be said, and do what needs to be done.

Martins' integrity as a man of God is of a calibre so very rare to find in this day and age, it is a privilege to see what God can do with and through a surrendered soul.

By reading 'A WRETCH LIKE ME,' you will find that your mistakes in a careless, brutal and unloving world are no match for the relentless love and sovereign power of our Lord and Saviour Jesus Christ. The promise of life is for all; regardless of where you have come from or where you are now...there is hope!

'A wretch like me' is a compelling true-life story that has and will continue to impact and change the lives of those who read it.

WAYNE MOORE, Pastor, Legacy Church,
London, UK.

It's my honour and privilege to endorse 'A Wretch Like Me' as well as the ministry of Martin Berry. This book will give you a real life encounter of an identity changed from a life of sin to a Son of God. Martin is an anointed man of God who has found his identity in Christ. He is not only anointed but is a man of honour, integrity and more importantly character.

DENVER THOMPSON, Pastor, & Founder,
Encounters Church,
Life Encounters International Ministries.
Northallerton, UK

This is the type of book that during the years I spent in prison I would search for. It is also the kind of book that I love to read since becoming a Christian as it keeps one strong in their faith. I have the honour of knowing Martin and his family first hand. They were instrumental in my walk with God and also in the two ministries I am associated with, Teen Challenge, and the E-gangs project. Martin is a true picture of Gods grace and ability to totally transform a life. This is a book I have been eagerly awaiting.

PAUL DAYES, Director, E-gangs project.
London, UK

Martin Berry is an engaging, vivid storyteller. When you add that to the fact that this is his own amazing life story, you have a riveting tale. And when you add the power of Jesus in transforming Martin, his wife, Sandra, and his sons into Christ followers who are truly making a difference for the King and his Kingdom, you have a blockbuster! You won't be able to put this book down. And when you have completed this story, you will give glory to God!

Dr. PAUL BECKER, Founder and President of
Dynamic Church Planting International
Oceanside, California, USA

Martin Berry is a pastor, a friend and most of all a man after God's own heart; with a colourful past and powerful testimony it demonstrates God's grace to save anyone, anywhere at anytime. All you have to do is say yes to Jesus and your life will be changed forever. He will then take you on an amazing journey as He has done for myself, Martin and countless others.

Dr. MARK VAN GUNDY, Pastor, Church of Destiny,
London, UK.

I am only one, but still I am one.
I cannot do everything, but still I can do something.
And because I cannot do everything,
I will not refuse to do the something that I can do.

- Edward Everett Hale

There is nothing noble in being superior to your fellow men.
True nobility lies in being superior to your former self.

- Ernest Hemingway

FOREWORD

I am privileged to have the opportunity to foreword Martin's first book. This book is been in the making for many years, which is an obvious thing to say. However, Martin has been sharing his life story with many people usually with audiences in the hope of helping many trust in the God that has walked with him since his life began. I have worked very closely with Martin over the past seven years in church and other Para-church cycles.

During that time I have come to know and admire the resilient spirit of a man who you are going to see unveiled in the pages of this book. With Martin, what you see is what you get. He has no pretence. He is very open and sometimes very vulnerable and this is demonstrated well in the story. He is always seeking to further other people's interests. He opens up his life to demonstrate just that. With this story he wants to spur many others toward God and to feel that we can triumph even though we have many struggles.

Martin I know to be very real. He takes everything that you would expect to keep someone down and brings pearls out of them. This is the kind of person Martin is. Always relaxed about hard things! In this I see his life parallels the words of Apostle Paul, 'If I must boast, I will boast of the things that show my weaknesses' that Christ may be glorified 2 Corinthians 11:30.

For me this is a great gift and appreciation of Martin. He has resolved to make his life count for Christ. It is with this vision in his heart that he continues to labour for the gospel wherever he goes. You will find this in the many encounters since his answer to the call to Christ in his life.

Martin has helped introduce Christ to many people. He is a fire starter. You cannot but catch the enthusiasm of Christ in him as he continues to dig up treasures in others. Most people, who don't feel they can be anything, change when they spend time in Martin's company. I have seen this replicated in many young lives that I was privileged to see with Martin and Sandra's leadership.

The very gift in him that the enemy wanted to destroy has now become the very tool he often employs to raise others up for God. I have no doubt that it was with this great gift of seeing good in others, that he planted his first congregation in London. I believe many other congregations will follow as he continues to set ablaze the love for Christ in people's lives, especially the backslider or those in the dregs! He is a no nonsense man!

I recommend highly this book not only to get to know the author, which is a given, but to be taken on a journey of a great, eclectic and entertaining true story. In my judgement it could easily be made into a feature film. However, the story will also help you discover the beauty of life that is given over to the Lord. This book will be a great success as a tool to witness the glorious riches of Christ.

CHARLES MUGENYI, Pastor, Woodberry Down Baptist Church London. UK

To my wife Sandra and my sons Aaron & Dean

In spite of all my fears and failures you always believed in me, and are an everlasting source of encouragement.

You were the reason God brought me home.

CONTENTS

CHAPTER ONE

UNORGANISED CHAOS

"Who you looking for?" The doorman asked. Pushing past him she scorned, "Never you mind!" She was only there for one reason, to see my dad! Their relationship was as good as dead, so she wasn't there for a friendly chat she was on a mission. She made her way to the rear of the building and found him with a group of friends' playing cards; there was a young woman, very likely a prostitute sitting on his lap. Mum was no longer in a rush, completely unruffled she strolled over to the kitchen area and took hold of a meat cleaver.

Calmly moseying back into the room where they were sitting and waiting patiently for her moment, WHACK! She brought the chopper down on his hand, severing three of his fingers. During the shock and chaos, which ensued, she rushed home while he was at the hospital having his fingers reattached. At a later date and in an act of revenge he returned to the house and coldly and calculatedly shot her three times in the legs at point blank range. He was subsequently sentenced to prison and mum commenced divorce proceedings. That's when I was born.

"Raised a Londoner"

It was 1968, and I was born at the Salvation Army Mothers' Hospital in London, which was eventually demolished in 1986. My hair was pure white and in the shape of a Mohican, and I was the apple of everyone's eye. We lived in the London area, and I attended an Infant and Junior School there. I was the youngest of five, three of us lived with mum, my brother and I together with my sister; my eldest sister lived with our grandparents in Liverpool, my fifth sibling was given up at birth, I've never met her.

My father was of Maltese descent and an RAF pilot, powerfully built with an enigma about him. He was a man of few words, an around-the-clock gambler and well-known hustler. On the rare occasion, he appeared at our house; he busied himself watching the horse racing on TV or disappeared into the toilet with the newspaper. If he wasn't at ours, you'd find him at his local betting shop or another one of his hangouts in the Islington area.

Things were financially tough at home, and although mum struggled, she worked hard to keep things afloat. I'd sometimes walk to Islington to see dad hoping to get some money. It was a six mile round trip from home, but the three-hour ramble there and back flew past, after all, I was expecting to get some dosh at the end of it. I loved the walk, it was another form of escapism for me; I just viewed it as a day out.

"It was like a scene from goodfellas"

The club was in the basement of a building on the main street; it had a very steep staircase leading down into a smoky dark hallway. Reaching the bottom of the stairs, I was quickly intercepted by a woman, "Who are you here to see?" I responded, "I'm here to see Teddy." She swiftly got behind me and softly but firmly pressed her hand into my lower back, quickly ushering me through a maze of halls and into a large room.

It was like a scene from Goodfellas an array of shifty looking men sitting around circular gambling tables. It was dark; smoke filled the air as I covered my mouth trying not to gag on the thick, unpleasant odour of cigarette smoke mixed with the stench of sweat and stale alcohol. Most of the men had their heads buried in their cards as if they were hiding from someone or something. I always wondered how they were able to see their cards with such low lighting and the thick smog that engulfed the room.

Quickly escorted through the tables, I remember catching the eye of this one man scowling at me. My eyes were fixed on him, as if in a trance, while I was being encouraged to keep moving. I couldn't seem to avert my eyes from his as I continually looked back at him while walking forward.

The lady firmly turned my head back to face forward while moving my hair out of my face and stroking my head softly. Still picturing that man, it was as if my mind was subconsciously committing to memory the lifeless dead look in his eyes and the defeated, dejected look on his face. I couldn't get it out of my mind. A warning of what was to come maybe?

I was taken into a back room near the kitchen area and promptly sat at a table. "You hungry?" She said while dishing me up a bowl of minestrone. I acknowledged her offer by eagerly nodding my head. The Maltese version of this soup was very thick with lots of meat, potatoes and vegetables, which came with a big wedge of uncut bread to mop it all up. I wasted no time getting it down me, as it had to last me the day.

After a while, my dad appeared from the dark greeting me with, "What are you doing here?" In his thick Maltese accent. "Dad, I was wondering if I could have some pocket money," he just sighed, reached into his pocket and took out some change. As he handed it to me, I quickly got the feeling he didn't want me hanging around, and after a brief exchange of words, he turned and left the room.

"She searched for weapons"

It was those little moments that chipped away at me, as my father turned and walked away. No emotion, no hug, and certainly no I love you. The lady then wiped my hair away from my face and said, "Come on; let's get you out of here," escorting me back to the front door. I had only ever called him dad when I saw him face to face because I was never sure if he wanted me to call him dad. On the surface, I put on a brave face, but it was having a serious knock on effect in my life.

On the way home, I bought sweets to cheer myself up, but still had a haunting picture of that mans miserable face in my head. I knew it probably caused trouble going to see dad, because not long after he showed up at our home. I'm not sure if it made him feel guilty, but I knew this: whenever he came round, it always ended badly.

So, fearing the worst, I deliberately made myself scarce. It wasn't long before trouble erupted. I ran into my room and sat on my bed with my knees pulled up and my arms wrapped around them. I buried my head into my knees and focused on the vibrations of their voices coming through the wall. It was the way I gauged things. My mind spun as I tried to concentrate on the sound waves coming through the wall, my heart was beating rapidly which made my breathing more erratic. It wasn't long before the vibrations got louder and louder, I began to hyperventilate as my heart raced.

Footsteps hurried out of the living room and into the hallway, so I rushed to the bedroom door and pulled it slightly ajar. Dad was leaving while Mum hurled threats at him as he rushed down the stairs, heading toward the front door. "If I die before you do, I am going to come back and f***ing haunt you. You jumped up f***ing Arab!"

When he came round, they always had aggressive verbal battles. There was something about him that infuriated mum, which often escalated into something more physical. When she reached boiling point she always searched for weapons - a can of paint, tables, knives, or whatever else she could lay her hands on. I'm sure she had a love for him somewhere inside, but their relationship was way too volatile and destructive.

I was always content when they were apart because they seemed much happier that way. Maybe this had something to do with mum's steadily increasing drinking habit, which you could see didn't agree with her. It was like Jekyll and Hyde when she had a drink, she'd be ok one minute, then explode at the slightest thing. I tell you, when mum was in a good mood, life couldn't be better, but when she wasn't that was a whole different story.

Mum was born in Liverpool one of ten children: five boys and five girls, she had a harsh upbringing. She met my Dad when she was very young and married him when she was only eighteen. My father was about twenty years older than her and apparently very well set up; although he went on to systematically gamble the family finances away, which left mum struggling for money. She was forced on many occasions to go looking for him to get money for food.

It was the 70's, and mum did a lot for our local community, organising Saturday cinema, showing movies on an 8mm projector at a house the council used for the benefit of local young people. She was a no nonsense go-getter, and people loved that. Home life was decent most of the time; mum busied herself doing odd jobs while trying to keep things afloat financially. One of her greatest traits was generosity; she'd give you the shirt off her back if she could, and always looked to help others. I learned never to tease a poor homeless person, as it was common to find that same person sitting at our dinner table later that day chatting with mum. She'd call us to the table, and we would eat dinner together with our new guest. It taught me good values and how to respect people who have hit rock bottom, or who are just having a hard time in life.

"He decided to beat his son all the way home"

My brother Billy and sister Susan although only a couple of years older than me, appeared significantly advanced in years because of the way they lived their lives. They were very similar in a way - they seemed very self-assured and worldly wise, whereas I was not so confident or secure. From a very young age, my brother Billy developed quite a reputation, as did my sister Susan. Her claim to fame occurred after she beat up a boy who lived around the corner. It caused quite a stir in our close-knit community; his dad (along with some locals) came round to have a word with mum.

Well, he was shocked to find out it was in fact, a girl who had given his son a good pasting and not a boy. In a state of humiliation and possibly feeling a degree of shame, he decided to beat his son all the way home. It was a funny sight, and I was glad it didn't escalate, as I know mum could have done something unthinkable.

My brother was zero tolerant, with a seriously short fuse; he carried that same sense of enigma as Dad did. I looked up to him, and I can honestly say he was my hero. I never saw him cry, even when mum beat him within an inch of his life. He had this steely hardness, very quiet and very self-assured. He took me on many adventures with his friends, climbing into old factory roofs looking for birds' eggs. I was terrified being on the local derelict factory rooftops, as we jumped across from building to building.

My brother and I did have one common thread; we were both pyromaniacs! We loved making fires, and that always got us into trouble. After starting one in our local park, the police were called and gave chase; my brother and a friend of his jumped into a nearby bush not realising they were stinging nettles. Another young kid and I got scared and decided to hand ourselves in; the two of us stood there as the police passed us by after discovering my brother and his friend. Standing there amidst the clouds of smoke and blue flashing lights our little innocent faces were covered in soot. We watched the police drag my brother and his friend away, relieved we didn't get caught.

"Why had they left me?"

For my brother, a good way to bring in finances, as a 9-year-old, was stealing Corona pop bottles from the local off-licence, and then sell them back to the store for 5p a bottle; 5p was big money in the 70's. So one sunny afternoon while out playing with my brother and his friends, I was asked to wait behind a wall inside the grounds of the local tube station.

I never knew why but decided to take the instruction nonetheless. I felt proud that my brother, along with his friends had entrusted me with a task. What an honour! I did my very best, trying to look innocent, and super cool at the same time, but it wasn't long before the police turned up, I hadn't even noticed. After all, I wasn't expecting them.

Without warning, I was suddenly grabbed by my arm and almost entirely lifted off the floor. I was rapidly dragged around the corner and into the high road. I looked up at the police officer staring straight ahead with a very stern and determined look on his face, screaming at him. "Let me go; I haven't done anything, let me go!" But, he wasn't having any of it. He barged me through a pair of doors and straight into a local shop. I was dangling on my tiptoes hanging from his vice-like grip as he proclaimed proudly, "Got him! The little runt."

I was baffled and was wondering where my brother and his friends had gone. Why had they left me? And why am I being held hostage and dangled in front of a shopkeeper and his customers for all to see? I twisted and turned trying to see where my brother was, but he had gone missing. I looked around the store and suddenly became aware of all the customers, staring at me with looks of immense disapproval on their faces. Trying to get my bearings I focused on the shopkeeper who seemed furious with me at that moment and looked as if he wanted blood. It was at that very moment a feeling of extreme helplessness, and isolation consumed me, then panic. My mind raced thinking, What if the policeman takes me away? Dad doesn't want me; my brother has abandoned me, who will come to get me? It was all too much. I started crying uncontrollably, and I got myself into a real state; I wanted to run, to escape, to break free.

"I hadn't realised I was the lookout"

I screamed as loud as I could while trying to yank myself free from the policeman. Twisting and turning, trying my utmost to get away I became hysterical, it was bedlam. The shopkeeper was shouting, the people in the store were murmuring, I was shrieking while trying to wrestle free, when suddenly I heard a loud but soft voice, "That's enough! Let him go!" Looking up, I saw a policewoman rushing through the doors.

Pulling in her direction, I could slowly feel the firm grip releasing. She made her way to me while reaching down to scoop me up. I ran straight into her arms and buried my head in her jacket; terrified at the thought of being taken away. She held me as I cried in her arms trying her best to calm me down. "It's ok, it's ok, shush, it's over now," she said softly. It was the only time I felt safe and secure. The policewoman took my hand and said; "I'll take it from here," she knelt down in front of me and asked where I lived.

Once that was established, she took me straight home and explained the whole situation to mum. The policewoman said it broke her heart to see me in such a state; she just had to bring me home. It came to light my brother, and his friends were stealing the Corona bottles from over the wall, but I hadn't realised I was the lookout. At that moment I didn't care, I was free, and that's all that mattered. Although I had come out of that situation relatively unharmed, it did hurt my confidence levels and left me with feelings of rejection.

You see I wasn't scared so much of the police taking me away, it was the thought of being left there with no one to come and get me. That scared me the most. My brother and sister always teased me saying, I'm not related to the family and that I was my Aunt's boy. On the surface, you could assume I wasn't bothered, but underneath it irritated the life out of me. It made me angry inside, but I had to accept it. After all, I couldn't physically do anything about it. Mum took us to visit her sister in another part of town so, rounding us up, we jumped on a bus and set off, it was like a mini day out.

It was great visiting close family; we didn't do it that often. Once there, mum told us to play while the adults spoke, we had no problem doing that. When the visit was over, mum shouted upstairs for my brother and sister to come down; I thought nothing of it at first, maybe she wanted to talk to them.

But after hearing voices in the hallway and the front door suddenly slamming shut, I jumped up and ran downstairs to find mum had left. She took my brother and sister with her. It was never explained to me why I was there, and I was too embarrassed to ask. So after a couple of weeks, I decided to make a break for it, and find my way home. With no money and no direction, I came up with a plan.

"I couldn't go home; I had no idea what to do"

While out playing I headed towards the high road to watch the buses, as they had the destination displayed on the front. Once I saw one that said Stamford Hill I mumbled, "That's near my home, I'll find my house from there." I then started to follow the route and kept reminding myself, as long as I follow the right bus, I'll make it home. And I did.

The strangest thing is, when I got there, mum wasn't so happy to see me, swiftly returning me back to my aunt's. The whole thing just confused me. Well, the hours, turned into days, which turned into weeks and I survived solely on the basis that my aunt was very loving and a relatively friendly person. She always reassured me, and conversations with her helped me process things a little better.

It wasn't long before that all wore off though, and I began to feel detached and lonely again. I was separated from my immediate family, with nowhere else to go. I couldn't go home; I had no idea what to do. I did consider running away, but again, the fear and feelings of abandonment held me back, because of that one prevailing thought in my head. Who would come to get me?

My auntie decided we'd all go shopping and during the day we ended up at a market. Tables filled with clothes and bric-a-brac were lined up with lots of people milling around. It was difficult trying to see everything because no sooner had you noticed something interesting your attention was stolen away by something else.

Perusing the stalls, I spotted mum in the distance, my brother and sister were with her. Suddenly, they vanished from sight through the thick crowds of people. My heart sunk, I thought they had gone. But they reappeared again. Fixing my eyes, I swayed to and fro trying to get a visual lock on them.

"Going it alone emotionally"

Fearing losing them in the crowds, I frantically called out to them; they saw us and made their way over. I was so happy, as I missed them so much. Mum got straight into a conversation with my aunt while my brother and sister were busy eyeing up the stalls. I looked up while they spoke, thinking the exchange would happen at any moment, and I'd soon be home.

The anticipation excited me so much; I played the scenario through my head a thousand times planning what to do once finally there. Waiting patiently for mum to finish her conversation, I took my hand out of my pocket waiting for her to take hold of it. The conversation ended abruptly, and she walked away with my brother and sister in tow, leading them away as they looked back at me. Part of me wanted to scream for them to come back, but another part figured it wouldn't make any difference.

Later that week dad came to my aunt's to visit; he had my brother and sister with him also. Just like the last episode, it was like I didn't even exist, no, "Hey son how are you?" He and my aunt chatted, as my brother and sister sat quietly on the sofa. I was seated in the middle of the living room floor watching TV on an oversized Persian rug placed in the centre.

I tried to concentrate on the television program but just couldn't; I was still trying to get my head around all this. Getting myself worked up made my head hurt, so I fixed my eyes on the intricate patterns on the rug trying to process my current situation. Reaching my breaking point of physical and emotional exhaustion, I kept asking myself, why is this happening? What's wrong with me? It was like a crazy reoccurring dream.

Drawn to my dad's voice I heard him say, "I think I may take these two swimming." I couldn't stand it anymore! Tears gushed from my eyes as I looked round from my isolated spot on the rug, "Dad please, can I come too?" He looked at me and replied: "Of course son." But he never reached out to me, just a cold yeah sure thing.

But, I needed more assurance than that, I needed to be held and told how much I was loved and wanted. That moment of emotional turbulence broke me. It made me realise I couldn't trust anything anyone ever said; survival for me meant going it alone emotionally. It wasn't long before a family domestic developed between mum and her sister, which finally brought me back home.

"Get her out here now!"

Things at home were steadily getting worse, Susan was dating now, and my brother was going out late at night and getting himself into trouble. Someone organised a house party not far from us, and Susan lied to mum saying she was staying at a friend's house, but, mum had a knack of smelling lies from a mile away and suspected something was going on.

Once she was completely sure, she acted upon it immediately. "Martin, get in here!" She shouted from the living room. Hearing her voice vibrate through my bedroom wall, I quickly got to my feet and responded. "Show me where this house is!" She bellowed.

I had a vague idea where it was and quickly told her. She swiftly put on her cardigan and grabbed me by the hand. We were now on our way to the house. Her feet were moving at such a high pace along the pavement I had trouble keeping up; she pulled me along adjusting my speed as she did.

As we approached the end of the road, and hearing the sound of loud music within the distance, I closed my eyes visualising the outcome, this wouldn't end well.

Reaching the house mum aggressively, and repeatedly, banged on the door shouting: "Where's my daughter? Get her out here now!" The door opened slightly, and you could just about see the figure of a young man behind it, "Who are you looking for?" He asked trying to look calm. Mum didn't like repeating herself, "I just told you, get her out here now!"

Realising the game was up, the guy slowly moved away from the door and Susan sheepishly appeared from behind it. Wasting no time, mum grabbed her long hair, and wrapped it around her hand while dragging her along the pavement. Susan tripped and scrambled along the floor screaming to be released. I hurried behind them trying to keep up as best I could while keeping my head down. It was humiliating!

Mum couldn't care less what anyone else thought; we were her kids, her responsibility. Back at the house, I hurried into my room, jumped onto my bed, and listened to the vibrations through the wall. The volume went up and down, but after a couple of door slams, the shouting stopped.

"Beatings became a regular occurrence for us"

My brother was a nomad, when he hung out with his friends no one knew what he was doing or where he was going. Lying in bed half asleep, I remember hearing him come into the room; we never spoke much, so I wasn't going to say anything to him. He carefully climbed into bed, and it went quiet. Some time had passed, and I could hear the faint sound of moaning & groaning coming from his direction; it didn't appear healthy.

I got out of bed, which was out of character for me and went over to check if he was ok, "Are you alright?" I whispered, "Go back to bed and leave me alone!" He replied. I knew something was wrong; I could just feel it. So I quietly stood there trying to go unnoticed. My eyes slowly adjusted to the dark, and then I could see the bloodstains on his covers.

He had his front tooth knocked out and had multiple stab wounds; embedded in his head were teeth from the combs used to stab him. He made me promise not to tell mum, we both knew it would cause unnecessary grief and would only make for more trouble. I agreed and went back to bed. If things weren't bad enough, Susan decided she'd had enough of mum and ran away.

She managed to keep a low profile moving around a lot, making it hard to track her down. She was missing for months and mum was now sick with worry. It was quite some time before we finally got news of her whereabouts. Someone had found out where she was staying and came round to tell us.

Mum wasted no time following up the lead, and after telling some family friends, they promptly apprehended her. I still remember my shock at her sight; the long hair that hung all the way down her back was now completely shaved off. The rest was dyed white with a green stripe down one side. I knew mum was furious, but gratitude superseded the anger, her daughter was safe, and that's all that mattered.

The stress combined with all the drama that went on in our home was apparently becoming too much for mum, and she started to derail. Her outbursts became more and more frequent, and she was becoming more physical; the beatings became a regular occurrence for us. I know her life was hard growing up, and dealing with us must have driven her to the edge.

She was so unpredictable you didn't know what she would do from one moment to the next; the anticipation of her outbursts frightened the life out of me. Whenever she raised her voice, it filled me with nervous energy and then panic. My brother just shook his head looking at me with disgust. He thought I was pathetic.

"Obviously, it wasn't the right thing to do"

The local church was taking us away for a week, which must have been a welcome break for mum; we all knew she needed it. It was one of those rare occasions that I saw my dad; who had come round that morning to see us off. But, as usual, something had to go wrong, and it did. None of us had any clean clothes ready, so mum got a load together and sent my brother and me to the launderette, which was at the top of our road. It was taking a long time, and mum's stress levels increased; she got into a state waiting for us to come home. I don't know if it was my dad's presence that made it worse, but when we got back, she went nuts; she shouted at us for taking too long and holding everything up. As she ran through the house trying to get everything together, I started to panic; this scenario was all too familiar.

While rushing around, she began to break down and then it happened. As I came up from the kitchen she met me on the landing at the top of the stairs and stood over me; I was terrified! I knew right then I was going to get it. Suddenly, dad came over and stood in between us. I knew that wouldn't help; I'd have to face mum when he wasn't around and would pay for it big time.

I had never been directly in the middle of a confrontation between mum and dad but experienced it from a distance. Dad was standing side on in front of me so he could keep an eye on us both. Mum wasn't happy at all with it and let him know, "Get out the way now!" Dad replied with a steely resolve, "You're not hitting him." For me, this was the unstoppable force meeting the immovable object.

She reached out to grab me, but dad quickly turned to face her creating a shield between us both; I stood back a few paces. They faced off, and that promptly escalated into a scuffle. Mum went berserk lashing out wildly as he tried to restrain her, crashing into the railings and walls on the landing.

Dad managed to push her away, but she lunged straight back at him pulling her fist back, he beat her to it swinging a right cross with bad intentions; the sound of his fist hitting the soft tissue of her face echoed around the landing and sent her flying across the floor. I had never seen my dad raise his fist until that day, and I never saw him do it again.

Mum lay motionless on the floor as he hurried us up, got us packed and out the door to the waiting minibus outside. No one on the bus was any the wiser, and as I sat there contemplating what just happened, the other kids jumped around laughing and joking. I remained silent...I thought he killed her. Driving away from the house left me confused. Surely I should be worried about mum lying unconscious on the floor, but no, I was relieved. I was playing the scenario over in my head, "What if she's dead? We could live with dad, that wouldn't be too bad." I couldn't muster any sympathy for her at that point, not one iota. After all, she was about to hurt me, so any love I had for her was slowly turning to resentment.

Living in a state of constant fear and worry caused me to consider the unthinkable. It was that type of fear that once made me consider stabbing her with a kitchen knife. For instance, she was preparing dinner and was stooped over looking into the oven when this feeling came over me; looking at a large knife on the kitchen table, a voice said, Go on, stick it in her, she'll never be able to hurt you again. Thankfully I couldn't, but that's where my headspace was. Obviously, it wasn't the right thing to do, and I knew that, but just couldn't endure the dread of her outbursts anymore.

Despite everything that happened I did love mum and wanted her to be happy, just without all the chaos. She had a great heart, and you would often catch glimpses of it in action, but something was holding her back. I must admit we were not entirely blameless in any of this; we did our fair share of misbehaving, which probably triggered her emotional outbursts. With that said and done, I still couldn't comprehend the manner in which she dealt with situations though, which nearly always ended in violence. It was the same with my brother and sister too.

"Why does it always have to come to this?"

During the summer, my cousin had come to visit, and we were playing in the nearby park located at the back of our house, when a lady casually strolled over picked up his three-wheeler bike and walked away. Calling out to her, we explained that it was not hers but indeed ours, she didn't want to give it back, positive it was her own son's bike. Seeing what had happened Susan confronted the woman who became quite aggressive causing Susan to dash home to tell mum.

Hearing what happened, mum instantly came to the park bringing Susan with her calling to the woman who was just leaving. Her kids' bike was identical to my cousins, and it was a simple mistake, but the woman was still seething at the way Susan had spoken to her and decided to give her a good dressing down in front of mum.

I knew that was a bad idea, while verbally laying into Susan she hadn't noticed mum picking up the bike while holding it in one hand. While the woman was still taking my sister to task, mum interjected, "So, you want the bike, do you? Well, have it then," launching the bike straight at her. With not much time to defend herself, she raised her hands as it crashed into her arms and face. I looked away thinking, why does it always have to come to this?

It was embarrassing the number of times I arrived home from playing out only to hear that mum had once again beaten someone up. Mums emotions were all over the place, and that's when she developed an unhealthy partnership with alcohol. The vicious cycle of excessive drinking then fits of tears and rage, quickly followed by smashing stuff and eventually living in regret. We all experienced that first hand one day, mum got herself into a real state screaming and lashing out.

Confused and scared we all desperately tried to get out of her way, but I got cornered. Grabbing me firmly by the back of my neck and trousers, she launched me at the metal coffee table in the centre of our living room. I dipped my head avoiding the top, but my knee crashed against the metal centre bar underneath it. Lying there in agony, I feared another attack. Susan dashed to her room, as mum set her sights on my brother. After a short scuffle, she threw him over the bannisters on our landing, and I still remember the horrific sound of his body hitting the stairwell below.

Mum collapsed to the floor crying and threatening to end her own life. Thankfully we came to know the priest whose vicarage was opposite our house; he was the one who took some of us away on a trip. I limped over to his house and told him what happened; he wasted no time coming straight over to offer support. Mum, obviously wasn't well and needed to be sectioned, and was taken to a nearby hospital, giving her time to get some rest. We fended for ourselves while she was away making the most of what we had at home. On her return, she was very apologetic and regretful. It broke my heart.

I was approaching my final years of junior school when I met a new kid named Darren; he just moved into the area from another country and was put in my class. Up until that point, I didn't have any real friends to speak of so having this close friend was a relatively new experience for me, and I was intent on maxing it out. That's when we came up with the idea...bunking off school, I never skipped school up until this point and was a little apprehensive, but once we got away with it a few times, the floodgates opened. In those days, you could buy an all day travel card for only 50p; it was called a Red Bus Rover and took us on some fascinating adventures.

"I quickly realised it was in trouble"

We liked the big shopping centres in and around London, which was my first real taste of freedom, and also my first experience of shoplifting. Mum taught us never to steal, and I didn't intend to at first, it just happened. We went into shops looking for Foster Grant sunglasses and fake gold chains, evidently unable to afford them; the temptation to steal over took me. But, that seemingly straightforward idea came to an abrupt end one sunny day in Essex; we were caught and arrested.

That experience put me off shoplifting, but left me with an enormous void to fill; I frequently felt empty. Being unable to cope with normality I started to form some harmful habits as a method of escapism, and I found that through sniffing glue and lots of it. I noticed my brother, and some of his friends were doing it; it seemed kind of cool.

My intention to go straight didn't last long, I now needed to fund my new habit, and that meant stealing again. So, one Saturday morning a friend and I went to Woolworths to pinch a 250ml tub of Evo-Stik glue, which fitted perfectly into a regular sized pocket. The 500ml tub was what I wanted but was just too bulky.

Scoring a tub, we'd either go straight into the local tower blocks or climb the fences onto the banks of the railway lines to sniff it. My mind was in a constant state of limbo, never fully sure which direction I was headed in, either running to something or away from it.

The idea of fitting in with society and living within the public norm confused me. I didn't even know what that looked like, let alone knowing what to do or which part I should even play. In this game of life, I worked hard to get noticed and was bent on making an

34

impression whether it was good or bad; I was full on with everything. I eventually succeeded in making a name for myself and was affectionately known as, "Gluey" in the local area. As far as I was concerned, that was great! I now had an identity. Of all the different places my friends and I went to sniff glue; the best had to be the railway lines. That was where the real adventure was.

"I was pretty wasted, staring into the sky"

We could go missing all day, and no one would know where to find us, acres of land, tall bushes and trees, the ground layered with grass, a panoramic view of south Tottenham with a mixture of passenger and freight trains frequently trundling through the picturesque landscape. We loved it so much we built ourselves a camp out there in the midst of a massive bush, easily thirty feet high.

We managed to hollow out the centre and furnished it with an old sofa, some broken car seats and a disused garden table. It was fantastic and provided me with just the right amount of disassociation I needed from my chaotic and often gloomy reality. Our new hideout had to be kept secret, as my brother was on the warpath with one of his pals, and caught a friend and me sniffing in the local flats, he wasn't happy at all.

He gave my friend a stark warning to keep away from me, and as he turned his attention to me, Billy's friend punched my mate full blast in the face, smashing his head against the brick wall, nearly knocking him out. I thought that was bang out of order! However, that experience didn't deter me, or my unfortunate friend; we were just getting started.

My sniffing got more intense as I became fully dependent, slowly developing into full on addiction; I was detached from reality and didn't want to come back. Getting the next hit of glue was all we thought about, and fearing my brother may be on to us, we avoided our base camp looking for a temporary place to sniff, and found it in the local flats not too far from where I lived.

It was a thirty-foot tower overlooking a taxi garage with a gravel drive leading to it, surrounded by concrete floors on all sides. The great thing was, I could see towards my house and into the flats, behind me was a clear shot of the high road, so if my brother showed up, we had many means of escape. On top of the tower, I could feel the heat of the sun beating down on me as warm air blew in my direction; the sky was clear bright blue with fluffy white clouds blotted all around. Clouds are always fun when you get high, they morph into different things and keep your mind occupied during the hallucination process.

I smiled to myself while pouring a generous amount of glue into a light freezer bag as the anticipation of this next high thrilled me. It wasn't long before I was pretty wasted, staring into the sky and interacting with it, probably conversing with those fluffy white clouds. I found myself facing the taxi garage, fixing my eyes on the gravel floor below. As I gazed down, the ground appeared as if it was coming up to meet me, then swiftly dropping back down again. So I closed my eyes.

"Cut on my head and a badly gashed leg"

I could hear a cracking and snapping sound, then a muffled voice; I opened my eyes, but could only see blurry shapes. I tried to wipe my eyes, but my arms weren't working! What's going on? I thought to myself, still obviously out of it. The sound of twigs snapping got louder, and my body made short, violent jerking movements. I opened my eyes again, but this time they managed to focus, I could just about see a person, but as I squinted to get a better look, I noticed the person was upside down.

Several sharp jerking movements later, I could hear the desperate voice of my friend, "What are you playing at man? What are you trying to do to me?" I could feel his hands under my armpits, and his voice bellowed behind my ear... A small birch tree planted below the tower had broken my fall, and my body was entangled in its branches. I passed out, falling nearly thirty feet off the tower headfirst into the tree.

If I had landed two feet to the left or right, I would have hit the concrete floor below and probably died on impact. As my friend frantically picked me out of the tree, he was in shock. I couldn't remember anything other than a terrible headache and the feeling of warm blood in my hair and around my body. When he finally got me free and sat me down, the feeling slowly came back into my body, and I was in real pain. I ran my hand down my leg, and I quickly realised it was in trouble. My jeans had been ripped from the top of my right thigh down to my ankle by a branch, and my right leg had a fifteen-inch gash in it, which was exposed.

We headed to the local A&E where I was promptly seen to, checked out and patched up. Surprisingly enough, there were no broken bones just a nasty cut on my head and a badly gashed leg. I think that was a defining moment for me, and a possible opportunity to give up sniffing glue.

I did give it some serious consideration but just couldn't stop. I promised myself each day would be my last, but that day never came. My sniffing partner decided enough was enough and he walked away leaving me to it. The glue was all I had left, and we continued on our unique journey together.

"Blood trickling through her fingers"

Billy was sent to find me, and as usual, he did. On the way home he informed me, "Mart, you're in serious trouble mate." While frantically trying to get the glue off my face, hoping I would sober up before reaching the house. He gave me clear instructions, "Say you were out playing with friends, and I found you in the local park."

That was the story, and we were sticking to it. Hoping for the best my brother gave me a heads-up, "Look, mum is already in a bad mood, so make sure you don't give her any excuse to freak out, do you hear me?" Waddling along the road, I yelled back at him, "Yes, ok, I hear you!" He just shook his head; I think he knew we were doomed.

Arriving at the house, I staggered into the living room and casually stood on the spot trying my best to look calm. Mum asked me sternly, "Where have you been until now you little s**t; you've been up to no good haven't you?" Remaining calm, I stuck to the story, "Mum, I was out playing with friends in the park and lost track of time." Thinking she'd bought it Billy quickly nudged me towards the living room door, in the hope of getting me to the bathroom in time to brush my teeth. But, as I turned to walk away she suddenly yelled, "Get here you, let me smell your breath." My heart sank; I closed my eyes and dropped my head. I turned slowly walking in her direction. Now faced with her, I feared the worst as my arms kept flinching to protect my face. She smelt my breath; then instantly grabbed my hair, pulled my head down and punched and kicked me repeatedly. My brother rapidly left the room, and it was Susan that wasn't so lucky this time.

Mum had got so mad, that in a blind rage she reached for a large crystal ashtray, sitting on a small coffee table in the centre of the room. She launched it straight at Susan, who wasn't expecting it. The ashtray hit her clean in the head. I turned away seconds before impact and remember the sickening sound of the solid crystal hitting her head. It happened so fast; Susan screamed jumping to her feet in shock as blood gushed out of her head.

She placed her hands over her face, and you could see the blood trickling through her fingers. I panicked too; she was hurt terribly and in great distress. Billy rushed to get the local priest, and he came swiftly. Mum got sectioned again at a local unit, and Susan was taken to A&E. I never understood why mum got herself in such a state, but I know the time she spent in hospital was good for her, although she was never fully healed. It would happen again, but this time she was the victim.

She was in fine form this particular evening, and everything was calm. While in bed asleep, the sound of screaming rang out; I woke up thinking someone had broken into our home. Quickly getting up I rushed into the hallway, but the screaming was coming out of mums' room. As I rushed in, she was lying on the bed screaming with a kitchen knife in her hand.

"I went over in a heap"

She had a gaping stab wound in her thigh. "Mum, what are you doing?" I shouted, "Mum, listen to me, hand me the knife," slowly and carefully reaching out and taking it from her. Once I had the knife, I wasted no time getting the priest who came straight over as usual. She was rushed to hospital, and to this day I still don't know what happened. My solvent abuse became a bit of a vicious cycle, and I genuinely wanted to stop. However, as mum kept having these episodes, I found it too difficult to deal with and used the glue to help me block it out. I was just too weak. I tried clearing my head by spending time with other kids in the neighbourhood, but while out playing the whispering started. They ran away from me. I wasn't in the mood to be harassed or laughed at, and just wanted to be alone, and I knew the perfect place, my camp over the railway.

So, I climbed a wall near the station and walked along the tracks, punting the big stones strewn either side of them, occasionally picking one up and flinging it into the distance. It was while sat on my backside after slipping on those stones, that I noticed an old shack in the distance. I never noticed it before and decided to check it out. It was an old workman's shed filled with dirty smelly Donkey Jackets. They were black and made of thick heavy wool with PVC shoulder reinforcements.

I tried one on and continued to rummage around the shed finding some old lamps and various tools. Eventually getting bored, I plopped myself down on an old metal pail. It was while sat staring into space that I noticed something peeking out from beneath an old cloth, deep in the corner of the shed.

Removing the material unveiled a great surprise; a five-litre can of Evo-Stik. I hit the jackpot! Grabbing hold of the can, I left the shack and quickly scurried around looking for a carrier bag, and found one in some bushes that had blown onto the lines.

Heading off to my hideout in amongst the woods, I couldn't wait to get started. It's always the same feeling, almost like getting ready to go on holiday when you are in a departure lounge; you have this sense of adventure and escape. Wasting no time and getting straight to it, I began to sniff in great quantity while looking around the dense and richly shrubbed area, trying to find a point of interest.

Several hours had passed, and being so distracted and inebriated, I hadn't noticed the amount of darkness, which engulfed my hideout. It was time for me to leave. The camp was pitch black, so using the moon to navigate my way out; I followed the railway tracks that were lit up, until I eventually reached the bridge. I then climbed down on to the main road and walked home from there.

When I got to my front door, I could hear the sound of music and voices coming from our living room window. Result! I thought to myself. Mum will probably be well oiled and distracted with her drinking partners to notice me. I let myself in; quietly tip toeing to the top of the stairs. There it was, my bedroom door. I waited patiently to make my move, but call it mothers' intuition or what, she came out of the living room right at that very moment.

She was understandably distraught and hurried in my direction shouting: "Where have you been until this time of night?" I just stood there covered in soot and grime, peeling the glue off my face. I calmly responded, "What? I haven't been anywhere!" She just stood there, I was confused, what, no shouting, no violence… BANG! With great force, she punched me in the stomach, and I wasn't ready for it; the sedation of the glue numbed the pain, but it couldn't stop me feeling the force of her fist crashing into my solar plexus.

I went over in a heap, and while lying on the landing floor I heard her voice echoing in the distance: "That will teach you, now get to bed!" I crawled along the ground, still winded and bent over from the punch. Getting to my room and climbing into bed, I lay there in agony feeling sick.

"Reflecting on my life"

The lights were off, but the moonlight gleaming through the window allowed me to see a strange figure in Billy's bed at the other side of my room, "Hello, do you want a hard gum?" He whispered; his mum was drinking in the living room too, which meant he'd be staying over. I felt ill at this point and sank my head back into my pillow replying, "Shut up, just leave me alone," while staring up at the cracks in the ceiling, trying to concentrate on the loose flakes of paint.

My eyes started to close, and I drifted into unconsciousness. Suddenly my slumber was interrupted! Opening my eyes, I was still in the same position but wasn't breathing; my eyes widened as I gasped for air, and my body lay powerless. Vomit spewed out of my mouth like an erupting volcano, as I coughed and gagged thinking this would be my end.

Then, without warning, my bedroom door crashed open hitting the wall, mum stormed into the room and hurriedly turned me over, while repeatedly smacking me on the back. I continued to vomit but finally managed to get my breath. Taking big gulps of air while staring at mum's feet beneath me, I could hear the sound of shock in her voice as it rang out, "Don't you ever take that stuff again, do you hear me?" We were in complete agreement, she wanted me alive, and I wasn't ready to die just yet either. That kid was lying awake in bed, and heard me choking. He then ran to get mum. I wonder if he was meant to be there that night?

That evening, I decided to leave the glue alone, and was genuinely serious about giving it up. I somehow had to get my life back on track, at least while I still had one. So, I managed to spend a little time reflecting on my future, and left the glue alone for as long as I could. Mum was still stunned considering how I could've died alone in that room, if it wasn't for that kid; that gave us plenty to consider.

"My face smashed into the railings"

But like most things in my life, it wasn't to last. Whenever I tried to get myself right, or abstain from getting high, another opportunity would present itself to me. Daryl came into my life as if out of nowhere. I knew him from around the way, but we were never buddies or anything like that. Somehow our lives were thrown together out of nothing... And he loved glue.

So after several weeks of abstinence, I was back on it again and losing my grip on reality. Not wanting to share my secret hideout with anyone, I took Daryl to a nearby train station instead. We climbed the spiked railings onto a steep railway bank, which led down to the tracks; it was late and very dark. Trudging through thick bushes and small trees, we found an open spot with just enough moonlight for us to see; and we made ourselves comfortable. While sniffing, I was fixated on the night sky as the moon and stars gave me plenty to work with while hallucinating.

However, I couldn't help notice out of the side of my eye that Daryl's facial expression was changing. I tried to take my mind off it, but it kept happening. I glanced over at him again, and without warning, he started to mutate into a werewolf, right before my eyes. I couldn't believe what I was seeing; I just stared at him in complete shock. Poor Daryl must have wondered what was going on, because as he got up to approach me, I darted up the railway bank crashing through the bushes while tripping on the undergrowth, running for my life. Hearing him scramble up the bank gripped me with terror, as the sound of snapping twigs and shrubs echoed behind me. Finally reaching the top of the bank with the werewolf still on my tail, the railings were now in clear sight. It was only then I realised; there was no time to climb over them without being caught, so thinking on my feet, I decided to jump... And I did.

While jumping headfirst over the railings, one of the spikes caught the pocket of my jeans, ripping them and stopping me in mid flight, I then swung down in a circular motion, as my face smashed into the railings, busting my lip wide open. Luckily the spike didn't puncture my hip, but pierced my jeans instead. I was dangling upside down looking back in the direction of the bank; and the werewolf was only feet away... I then passed out.

I came to, hearing the sound of Daryl's voice yelling at traffic for help. A car stopped, and two Rastafarians came over to lift me off the railings. They laughed as Daryl tried to explain to them what happened as the got me free. I needed to stop this crazy habit, and find something safer to do.

"Susan began screaming and bolted"

Strangely enough, it was around this time that dad started coming to the house. Not once or twice, but every day. Morning after morning like clockwork, he showed up early and left some sweets on my bedside table. One particular morning he tried to wake me up, but I was just too tired, I did try to make an effort, but he decided to leave me alone. Making sure I got to bed early that night I was incredibly excited intent on surprising him the next morning. I kept waking up and checking my table, I didn't want to see the sweets and miss dad, so I lay back and eventually fell back to sleep.

Waking up early that morning, I glanced over at my table, and it was still bare. There were no chocolates, so dad couldn't have been already. Still excited, I jumped out of bed and grabbed my clothes to get dressed. That's when I heard a knock on the door, it's dad, he's here! Throwing my clothes on as fast as I could mum headed downstairs to answer; I wanted to make it up to him for yesterday. Standing behind my bedroom door, listening to his footsteps coming up the stairs, I prepared to jump out and surprise him. They were now at the top of the landing. So I eagerly rushed out the room, wait; it's not my dad, but his brother Charlie. Sensing something was wrong; I stood in the middle of the landing, taking turns watching mum and uncle Charlie, occasionally looking back at the stairs for dad to arrive. But he didn't. Turning back to my uncle, I watched as he slowly took off his trilby hat, and meekly lowered it to his chest, while he wiped his face with his other hand.

He stared at the floor for a few seconds, and then looked up at mum. "Teddy's dead, I found him on the stairs at his home. He had a heart attack." My mind erupted, NO! I'm awake now; I'm awake, I want to talk, I want to talk. My mind went into overload, and then abruptly broke. Mum burst into tears, as Susan began screaming, then bolted into her room. Billy and I stood frozen in time.

Dad's funeral arrangements caused many arguments between mum and her family. But besides all that mess, his funeral was great - there was so much respect paid to him. It never fully hit me that he was gone, until we arrived at the crematorium. It was when his coffin started to depart, and the curtains slowly closed, then the loss sank in, and I finally cried. Susan never entirely recovered from his death, and it was going to have a lasting effect on her.

Several weeks later Billy had enough, and without a word, he packed his bags and disappeared into the night; we didn't see him again until he was a lot older. Those times had to be the worst for me, as I was the only one in the house when mum broke down in tears and cried hysterically. There was to be a little light at the end of this very dark tunnel.

It came to light that mum was seeing an Italian lorry driver named Lino (pronounced Leeno). He was born and raised in the north of Italy in the Piedmont mountain region. He was short and looked like the actor Charles Bronson. She tried to keep him a secret but realised she'd eventually have to introduce him to us. I believe he came into our lives at the perfect time.

Although the situation was a little raw for me, I could see how well he treated mum and he was actually very nice. He worked as a long distance lorry driver, which meant he travelled a lot, giving mum the opportunity to go with him, which she did. She loved it! You could see a significant difference in her disposition; she was a lot calmer and happier when he was around.

Lino got his first taste of mum's anger, as he was present when she took off on me. Being new to this situation, he decided to get in between us. I'd been in this position before, and was well prepared for the outcome. But, it didn't go as I figured it would. He didn't raise his fist or his voice, but quietly and confidently told mum the way she dealt with things wasn't helpful, then, she started.

"I travelled from country to country"

As they argued, I felt sick inside. The same old feeling of abandonment and isolation came flooding in, I was sure he would leave us, and we'd never see him again. I was desperate for him to stay. I was sick of being in the middle of these horrible situations; my emotions were in tatters. I tried to come to terms with the prospect of losing him, but wasn't going to wait around for the outcome. So I ran into my room and sat there crying.

A little while later there was a knock at my door, nobody knocked on doors in my house, so I didn't know how to respond. The door opened, and Lino walked into my room, gently sitting on the end of my bed. With a limited amount of English, he asked, "Martin, listen to me, if you want me to leave I will, just give me the word and I'll never come back." For the first time I was given an opportunity to decide the outcome, it was my choice to make.

I wanted him to stay for good. So, wiping away my tears, I plucked up the courage to tell him how I felt. Slapping his thighs, he jumped to his feet and yelled; "It's settled then," giving me a big hug. I can't begin to explain what that felt like, it made all the pain go. Taking me by the hand, he led me out onto the landing and called for mum.

She came rushing out of the living room wondering what was going on. He asked her, "Can we get Martin a passport?" With an inquisitive look on her face, she questioned why. He then said, "I want to take Martin on the road with me, I think it would be good for him." I genuinely thought there was no way mum would ever allow that, but to my surprise, mum said casually, "Sure, we can get him one now if you like? Let me get my shoes." I was in a daze! Mum then took me to the main Post Office on the high road, and bought me a yearly passport; I was beside myself with excitement.

As a taster, Lino took me to cities all over England, allowing me to see many interesting places. I was very excited at the prospect of leaving England; I'd never travelled before, more importantly, with someone that wanted me around.

Lino and I travelled from country to country, spending weeks on end relaxing in Italy where he lived. He was an incredible person; always encouraging me and making me feel important. Some of the places I got to see were amazing! The mountains in Italy were colossal, the roads were winding and very intimidating, no barriers to stop you from going over the edge.

The height was terrifying, but the scenery was breath taking. It was so much easier to get things into perspective in Italy, and I could relax, as nobody knew me, and I could be myself. When Mum came over to join us, she was always in a good mood, and occasionally let her hair down. Lino knew how to get the best out of mum, and it was so good to see her happy at last.

"Guys kicked her full blast in the face"

Back home, Susan was spending time with a guy who had a bad rep, and his brothers were bad news too. Mum and Lino had gone out for the evening into central London, while we were all tucked up in our beds. Sometime during the night, Billy and I were awakened by sounds of screaming coming from outside our house. Billy jumped out of bed to see what was going on.

Looking out the window, Billy gritted his teeth, "s**t!" Grabbing his jeans and trainers trying to get them on while heading out the room; five men were attacking mum and Lino outside our house. I jumped out of bed and desperately clambered around the floor to find clothes. We ran onto the landing, met by mum racing up the staircase screaming, "Get the police," while spitting blood.

She promptly turned and headed back down the stairs and back outside. My brother and I followed behind her. Lino was laying face down unconscious on our footpath while mum was standing in the middle of the road surrounded by these guys, my brother headed out into the street to help her, but turning towards him she shouted, "Get back in the house now!"

Right at that moment one of the guys kicked her full blast in the face, she had no time to defend herself and was sent crashing to the floor. I blanked out at that point. I was in total shock. The ambulance arrived, and the medics came into the house. Mum had lost most of her teeth, which had been kicked out, Lino came round; he had a pretty severe concussion from being hit over the head with a metal bar.

When the police finally arrived to take statements, it came to light that Susan knew one of the men. They were trying to rob mum of her jewellery, and she wouldn't give it up. Once we established who it was, it was straightforward to sort out. And we'll say no more about that.

"Carol may have been in a fight"

Susan had made a new friend named Carol, who at the time was aspiring to be a model; they had become good friends through CB radio and were hanging out at a local club. They were friends for quite a while so she asked Susan if she would like to move in with her; She was renting a studio flat in a converted attic on the top floor of a three-storey house.

At the time, we thought it was an excellent idea; mum was finally chilling out, Billy was living his life, and I was doing a lot better too. It seemed to be the perfect scenario for our family. Plus, it would give Susan a little independence, and that couldn't be bad.

On the day of the move, mum invited Carol round for afternoon tea to meet our family, and then we'd drop Susan's clothes round to her flat. But, the evening came to a close, and Carol hadn't shown; we were all a little concerned. Maybe she got cold feet. After waiting some time, Lino and I took Susan round to the house, and left her at the foot of the stairs leading up to the front door.

She brought her bags just in case. Lino and I travelled to Birmingham that night and left straight away. We got back later that evening to see flashing blue lights, and numerous police cars lined up outside my house; I thought something was wrong with mum. Still wondering what was going on, I rushed through my front door and swiftly made my way upstairs.

Mum was in floods of tears, and met me at the top of the landing. They were different tears than any I'd seen before; there was a difference. Trying to get her words out, I only managed to catch, "Susan" and, "Dead"! Fearing the worst, I ran into Susan's bedroom only to find her cowering under the covers. When I pulled back the covers, I saw the look in her eyes, and it was disturbing! She started screaming hysterically, so I quickly dropped the covers. I still needed to find out what was going on, and went to find mum, she was in the living room giving the police a statement.

"I was growing up"

Police officers filled our home, which told me it must have been bad; someone had murdered Carol, that's why she hadn't made it to our house that afternoon. When Lino and I had left earlier, Susan let herself in and went straight to their room at the top of the house. Carol was in bed; Susan thought she had probably slept in and left her to it.

About an hour had passed, and Susan became a little concerned, Carol hadn't moved an inch, so she began checking on her. As she approached, she noticed her hair had big clumps missing, so she thought Carol must have been in a fight. Susan pulled back the covers and what she saw terrified her. Carol was lying on her back with her eyes wide open, looking straight up at the ceiling.

She had been strangled, and was severely beaten; Susan said she didn't remember much else, only that she had to get down six flights of stairs and out the building, knowing the killer could still be in the house. Soon after that ordeal, calls were made to our home from someone proclaiming to be the killer, saying he would come to get Susan too. I once picked up the phone and heard him speak. Man did that get me angry!

The police decided it would be a good idea for us to move to another location, as they never caught the killer. Susan couldn't cope, and agreed to go to Liverpool to stay with family. I spent so much time on the road, I forgot about secondary school, and that made me apprehensive. The transition from junior to senior school was quite nerve racking for me, but it had to be done. Billy and Susan took me for a tour of the school, and I felt better prepared.

Mum got me ready early in the morning, combing my hair tightly across my head, as she forcefully gripped my chin bending my head from side to side. I looked dapper. She bought me the full school uniform, so I was well turned-out, and equipped for my first big day too. Morning assembly was the first major meeting of the day, I felt a little intimidated, but the excitement of the unknown outweighed my feeling of uncertainty. I was finally growing up.

"Come here and don't run"

The assembly hall was massive. There were so many people, the newbies, the first years, and the hard-core regulars; it was easy enough to identify who was who. Mum was quietly confident that I would be ok with Billy and left us to it. The minute she left, Billy and one of his friends gave me a sixty-second makeover. They rearranged the tie that was skilfully arranged around my neck, making it short and stubby. Opening the top button of my shirt, and messing up my hair.

I was now ready for the big bad world of senior school. The day went as well as could be expected, I wandered around the playground looking for other lost newbies to affiliate myself with, but didn't have much luck. I decided to take my search inside. Feeling a little excluded and very isolated, my mind switched from looking out for possible friends to foes. Those typical school bullies who would be out stalking the likes of me. There was no action inside the building; so I figured I'd take my chances outside.

The school grounds were crammed with young people, wandering through the bustling crowds trying to fit in. I noticed a group of guys sitting on a wall to my right; they were my brother's age or a little older. Fearing being spotted, I swiftly made a sharp left turn to avoid them. "Oi, you!" One of them snarled, I pretended not to hear him, but my natural response made me look in their direction.

"Yeah, you!" He yelled pointing his finger right at me, "Come here and don't run, or we'll come after you and do you over." It was just my luck! This kind of thing always happened to me. I honestly wondered if there was a sign on my head saying bully me. My heart raced as I walked towards them; I felt extremely vulnerable. "What's your name?" One of them inquired.

Taking a deep breath, I replied, "Martin," he thought I was trying to be funny and said sarcastically, "Martin what?" So I said, "Berry." No sooner did that name leave my lips, murmuring started among them. The same guy then asked, "Do you have any brothers?" I figured they might know him, "Yeah Billy," I said confidently.

"Where have you been today?"

He suddenly lost interest in me, "Go on; you can go," he said, turning his back to me as he faced his friends. I stood there in shock, wondering what just happened. Then, one of the others motioned to him that I was still there, and that concerned him even more. He spun round with more seriousness in his voice and said, "I said go! Get out of here, scram!" It felt great! I walked away feeling invincible.

In the end, it didn't amount to much, other guys who didn't know, or even care who my brother was, bullied me regularly. Worrying about the trouble it would cause if my brother found out, actually made me nervous. I just knew there would be retribution. My home life had trampled the fight out of me, and I was just too jittery to stand up for myself.

I got to the point where the very thought of violence made me feel sick. I couldn't take any more of the bullying at school or what would happen if mum or Billy found out, so I decided to go missing. At first, I skipped a day here and there, but eventually decided to go all the way, and left altogether. I spent my days hanging out in the local neighbourhood, or took a long bus ride around town.

It was quite some time before mum finally found out I hadn't been to school; I wore my uniform every day to throw her off, but the game was up. Mum was waiting for me to get home and sat in the kitchen, when I arrived she asked me calmly, "Where have you been today?" I replied confidently, "I've been to school mum."

No sooner had I finished my sentence, she grabbed me by my tie, pulling it so tight it ended up in a little knot, which started to strangle me. Dragging me into the bathroom, she somehow managed to get my tie over the door and yanked on it hard. I felt my feet leave the ground as my tie trapped my neck.

I was trying to scream with the little amount of breath I had left, "Help me! Help me!" Fortunately, Billy managed to jump in between us both and got her off me. My school tie was so tight that it disappeared beneath my skin; Billy had to cut it off so I could breathe. Taking big gasps of air, I was relieved to be alive. As always the local priest came and he was a great help.

"I was relieved to be alive"

I made a real effort to fit in at school, but it was so hard sitting in class with everyone observing me, that strange kid who doesn't fit in. Trying to focus on the lessons was impossible; I was just too far behind. Seeing as I couldn't understand the lesson plan, how was I meant to know any of the questions, it was a real burden and made getting up in the morning demoralising.

I got migraines regularly because of the pressure, and the pain was so bad that sometimes I'd cry myself to sleep. The whole school system depressed me. I repeatedly got into trouble with the teachers at school, because of my inability to learn, and was sent out of class for not complying, the trouble was I didn't know what I was meant to be complying with, so it was inevitable I'd be excluded from class; and that happened frequently.

I finally ended up in The Unit, a place where they kept all the outcasts who couldn't get along. Oddly enough, there was a vast improvement in my behaviour, and an output of work during my time there. I think being able to learn at my own pace, and according to my own cognitive ability helped me gain some confidence.

Every morning we were rounded up into the unit, locked in and forgotten about until break time. Once I had served my time there, the school tried to integrate me back into the mainstream. But, it just didn't work. They finally agreed I couldn't cope in that environment, and looked at other avenues for me. I had the option of a home tutor too, and that seemed like a good idea; she lived near our home and appeared very friendly. Her methods were unique, and she was very knowledgeable. She was very patient with me, and I learned a lot from her, although she did have a child who wanted constant attention, and that proved to be a hindrance.

As always, getting distracted, I wandered off into my own little world and slowly began to lose interest. This situation caused problems at home again, and we had to have a meeting with the Education Welfare.

"I felt like a lab rat"

They sent me to a particular school, and things settled down. I did get on with my work but again, there were too many distractions for me; kids who didn't want to work and disrupted everything. It was all made worse by a teacher taking an instant dislike to me, singling me out, while another picked up on that and overcompensated for it by being extra kind to me.

The truth is, neither helped - I just wanted a normal school life and was happy to get on with it. A referral came in for me to see a psychiatrist; they thought something was mentally wrong with me. I was put through a variety of tests to measure my thought patterns, while they desperately tried to figure out what made me tick.

I felt like a lab rat, sitting there as they examined me; it made me feel stupid and brought me to tears. I wasn't coping mentally and didn't care what happened to me anymore. I decided never to return to school, no matter what! I'd die before they made me go back.

A school for delinquents was my final destination, and it wasn't too far from where I lived; it was well known. You had to be a desperate case to get in, so I passed with distinction. Believe it or not, I flourished; even mum was relieved to see my school life improve. Our relationship improved too. I was finally starting to get a sense of worth at this place, and it was one of the best experiences in my school life

CHAPTER 2

BEER, SKATES & BREAKS

We finally moved house when I was thirteen years old, and put the death of my dad and Susan's ordeal behind us. I tried to settle in at our new home, but maintained the friendships from my old area. Mum was spending the majority of her time in Italy, which left me alone in the house for months on end; it was awesome though, as I enjoyed the peace. But being on my own, I got easily bored and started to experiment with alcohol. Almost every night I went to the off-licence to buy the strongest lager I could get my hands on. At that time it was Tennent's Extra Strong, I'd also buy a bottle of Thunderbird to help wash it down.

"I could save and steal a little"

I spent that Christmas alone and had blown all my food money; so Christmas morning there was just enough money to buy a chocolate bar at the local petrol station. However, In the New Year, one of my pals came to see me bearing gifts (two cases of beer) to end the year appropriately. We spent the entire night watching an endless amount of cheesy 70s and 80s music videos, while downing cans of Tennents super strong lager.

We were well into the next day and had finished all the lager. It was almost daylight, and we were both smashed! There were cans sprawled all over the front room floor; you couldn't even see the dustbin. Desperately needing a distraction from my excessive binge drinking, I fortunately found one.

It was evening, and I was sitting in the local park having a drink, when I heard the sound of loud music booming from the park entrance, I could also hear the sound of voices in the distance, so I went over to check it out. There was a mixture of guys and girls, some skating around, while others sat talking. Being all the more intrigued, I got closer to see what was going on, and suddenly noticed they had taken the cover off the local streetlight, which they had wired up to their ghetto blaster. Talk about free enterprise.

It was roller hockey, and all the rage back then. Pretty much the same as ice hockey, but with roller-skates. I noticed a couple of friends within the crowd and moseyed over to investigate more. One of them brought a fresh pair of Bauer Turbo's, and they looked awesome on him, which got me thinking, could a pair of these big black boots with leg warmers wrapped around them make you look cool? I decided to get a pair by saving my alcohol money. It was weeks before I could save and steal enough to afford them.

Making some new skater friends was a different experience for sure; they didn't know my family, or me, so that meant I got a fresh start. One of the guys in the group agreed to take me to get my boots; he was older than me and wanted to make sure I got the right deal. We jumped on a tube at the local station, and chatted all the way there, he assured me that getting the skates was the right decision, and joining the crew was too. It was all a bit strange for me; I didn't know these guys from a bar of soap, not to mention, I couldn't skate to save my life; nonetheless, it seemed like a good idea at the time.

"A taste of 80's street justice"

My circle of friends had completely changed, and that affected the way I interacted with people. My skating skills improved dramatically, and it wasn't long before I developed a reputation as a bit of a lunatic, jumping off staircases and walls nearly wrecking my skates in the process. They decided to start a hockey team and it sounded cool, but I figured to get in, I would have to earn my stripes. But, to my surprise, I was embraced and soon taken to get my team jersey and a stick.

Hockey stick in hand, and wearing my new jersey, I quickly got to grips with the game, and learned how to use my equipment. Little did I know I'd be using that same stick to break bones. Once the team was established, we trained in the park, as well as the basement garages underneath the local tower blocks, I quickly realised that being part of this crew had its advantages.

Two guys from the local neighbourhood pickcd a fight with one of our crew, that information then trickled back to the neighbouring streets. I had just left my house and was on my way to meet up with the guys, when I walked right into the commotion. I tried to gather enough information to figure out what was going on, but with all the disorder and hostility, it was pretty hard to make out. Suddenly, one of the crew came skating erratically towards us, and man was he animated. "We've found them!" He shouted loudly, "Some of the others are with them now," he said, while doubling back as we all followed after him.

"Wrong place, and the wrong time"

We rushed down to the estate as fast as our skates would carry us; I was a little behind, and took that time to prepare myself for the confrontation. My friends had trapped the two of them in the local estate, and had them surrounded. By the time I got there, they had already disappeared below the crowd of angry guys pounding them to mush, with a combination of fists, boots, and hockey sticks.

I got stuck in, handing them a taste of 80's street justice. While they were being beaten, I caught a glance of a bloody disfigured face, and he suddenly started hysterically screaming my name, "Martin, it's me! I'm sorry, please, please! We were at junior school together." I panicked and didn't know what to do. I yelled at the top of my voice, "F***ing leave him alone, stop it! Aimlessly grabbing my friends, trying to pull them off.

I continued yelling, "Stop, leave him alone, he's had enough, he's had enough!" Some were left puzzled as I tried to stop them; it was all too much for me. Hearing him scream my name for help did my head in. I threw my stick to the ground and covered my ears to block out the sound, and skated away as fast as possible. I didn't stop until I reached my house.

I rushed inside, kicked off my boots, and ran up to my room, slamming the door behind me. Landing face down on my bed, I grabbed my pillow and pulled it down firmly over my head; I was trying to get the picture of my friend's badly beaten and bloodied face out of my mind. The screaming continued in my head for hours, until I finally managed to nod off.

During the night, I woke up and couldn't get back to sleep. What bothered me the most was, that screaming kid was certainly not a bully or even a wicked person. I knew him. Talk about wrong place at the wrong time. Guilt followed me everywhere, but although I tried to justify it, it wouldn't shift. I wasn't cut out for this kind of stuff, and was in two minds whether to leave the group or not. But the decision was finally made up for me.

"My forearm looked like an s-bend"

Underneath a local tower block, we played a game like Pac-Man; chasing each other through the maze of corridors, trying not to get caught. While flying down one of those passageways, moving at high speed, I crashed into someone, sending me head first off a five-foot stairwell. While in mid-air, I instinctively reached out my hand to protect my head, and felt a snap!

My head hit the floor regardless, as I crashed into a heap on the solid concrete below. It took a while for me to get my bearings, as I was completely dazed. Feeling nauseous, I looked down at my hand; which was now numb, and began turning a funny colour right before my eyes. I knew it wasn't good and shouted, "My arm, it's broken!" One of them came over and stared at me blankly, "It can't be, you wouldn't be sitting there like that if it was, you'd be in serious pain." This stuff wasn't new to these guys; they had seen this sort of thing many times over, deep lacerations, abrasions, bumps and bruises, even stitches too.

So there was no sympathy for me. Wearing a leather jacket with a sweat top underneath, meant you couldn't see any damage. As long as I was still breathing, and there was no physical sign of injury, complaining just implied you were a wussy. No one offered any help, and they left me to skate to the hospital on my own. But it was just too painful; swinging my arm back and forth hurt way too much. A bus came along, so I jumped on it and headed to the hospital.

The drive there was bizarre, so many people gawked at me, wondering why I was on a bus wearing skates, which made me feel slightly stupid and embarrassed, it was a little hard to take. Arriving at the hospital, I went straight to A&E and told the reception what happened, they took me in immediately. I didn't think it was too severe, as the pain had lessened in my arm, and my hand was now entirely numb. They put me on a gurney, wheeled me into a cubical, and parked me next to a mother with her young daughter having her finger stitched; the poor girl cried her eyes out as they closed the cut on her little pinkie.

They took my jacket off first, then my jumper, no way! My forearm looked like an S-bend. Both bones just behind my wrist had completely snapped, leaving my wrist hanging and my hand limp. The little girl instantly stopped screaming, while looking at my arm in awesome wonder. I looked over at her and just shrugged my shoulders putting on a brave face. The nurse wasted no time trying to put it in a splint, which was difficult as my arm was crooked.

"I felt so humiliated and was furious"

Mum was in Italy at that time, so I was on my own. They rushed me into theatre, reset my arm and stuck me in a ward to recover. Later that same night, I woke up in severe pain as the morphine wore off. I was rushed back in again, because one of the bones in my arm hadn't knit together. I was eventually taken to see a bone specialist, and he decided to put a plate across the bones and screw them together.

However, later that evening, my hand blew up five times its standard size, and the nurse was called; the swelling was causing my hand to burst through the plaster. Again, they rushed me back into theatre, put another plate across the other bones and screwed them together also.

There was a shortage of beds in the recovery ward, so they moved me to a psychiatric ward at a hospital near my home. Mum had returned from her travels and must've wondered where I was; she somehow found out and came to see me every morning. After six weeks of treatment and therapy, I was finally free to go home. That's when I got the news, not only was my brother Billy moving back in; he was also bringing his new girlfriend with him.

I figured the company wouldn't be that bad at first, but discerned what would soon come of it. Being a 15 year old and keeping myself organised was a task in itself, but trying to compete with my older and somewhat crazier sibling, was a more daunting prospect. When mum left, he took control of the finances, and eventually full control of everything. After several months alone I had developed a pretty good routine, and hadn't realised it was about to come to such an abrupt end.

It started on our first shopping trip; we were scouring the aisles looking for something interesting for dinner, as well as some snacks for in between. Seeing one of my favourites, I quickly reached down and grabbed it, preparing to throw it into the trolley. Billy shouted abruptly, "Put that back, we're not having those!" It was his first time shopping with me, so I thought I'd help him along, "But I always buy some of these," I said assertively dropping them into the trolley...

Whack! "Well, you're not now, are you?" He said flinging the packet into the side of my face, while casually walking off with the trolley. I felt so humiliated and was furious; it was in full view of other customers in the store. The only good that came out of that moment was the shame, which covered the pain in my face.

"Nearly knocked me unconscious"

Billy was now running things in the house, and our relationship rapidly broke down. The milkman delivered our milk back in those days, and the money had to come out of the house funds. So when the milkman came to collect, there was no one around to pay, so I paid it out of my pocket, intending to get at least half of it back from Billy or his girlfriend, as I was barely using any. He wasn't around at that time, so I told her I paid it, and she gladly gave me half the money.

News of a party in the area got out, so needing to let my hair down, I quickly contacted some friends, and we headed over to it; we had a great time and got back super late. I forgot my house key and decided to climb in through the front room window; we had Louvre windows with toughened glass, so it was easy to slide the blades out then back in again. After climbing into the house, I replaced the glass and came back inside. The sound of footsteps echoed from upstairs, and my brother rapidly intercepted me. "Where's my girlfriend's money?" He shouted.

Shrugging my shoulders I answered: "What money?" He didn't like my response: "Say what one more time, and you'll see." So I paused, then repeated it, "I don't know what you mean, what money?" With a frustrated look on his face, he spun around and disappeared upstairs. Sensing his return, I waited on the spot; he came back down brandishing a broken snooker cue.

"Leaving home at a very young age"

I stood there for a second and thought to myself, he means the money for the milk right? But that's not her money. Without any consideration he launched at me with this lump of wood, swinging it indiscriminately. I raised my left arm to protect my head, (my right arm was still in plaster) the stick cracked the top of my hand, and the pain was excruciating!

As the next swing came, I couldn't raise my left hand and took a blow to the head; it caught me flush with incredible force and nearly knocked me unconscious. He took another swing, and I had no choice but to put my right arm up to protect myself. By the time he finished hitting me, the plaster on my arm was like mush. Looking up from the floor, I watched as he casually turned and walked away, heading back upstairs with the stick resting on his shoulder.

Feeling humiliated, I slowly made my way upstairs and into my room. My arm was limp, and my head was killing me, but I managed to settle down eventually and sleep it off. I got up early that morning and left money on the table for the bill, then headed straight to the hospital. When I got there, they asked me what happened, so I lied through my teeth. Luckily without any more questions, they gladly gave me something for my head, and re-plastered my arm.

I suppose things at home could've been worse, after all, we did grow up in the same crazy house. He had scars to prove it too. He broke both his legs and his arm crashing a friend's motorcycle into a lamppost at high speed, which left him with a severe limp. He was also charged with murder and received an eighteen-month prison sentence for armed robbery with aggravated assault. Now that's quite a lot for a young teenager to get through.

CHAPTER 3

THE LAND OF DRINK AND MONEY

It was the summer of 1983, and these were the feel-good days, with long hot summers that seemed to last forever. It was at this time break dancing & body popping swept the UK. It exploded onto our television sets, appearing on nearly every program from breakfast TV to evening music shows. It looked cool, and the music wasn't bad either. Being an inquisitive 15-year old, I was obviously well interested.

I saw an advert for a newly released movie called Flashdance, and went to the local cinema to watch it. Entering the foyer, I saw a large assortment of young people, all in groups (crews) talking amongst themselves while checking each other out. They were there collectively for one reason; this movie had some break dancing in it. While hanging around, I got talking to a guy named Mark, an 18-year-old Jamaican, who lived just around the corner from me. We got on straight away; he was easy to talk to and a good laugh. We hung out during the movie and really enjoyed ourselves.

As we left the cinema, I told him to come round to my house whenever he wanted, but figured he never would. Later that week there was a knock at the door, and it was Mark. One thing I did notice was that he was very muscular and looked like he did weights. I got on to him about taking me to the gym, but he just wasn't interested in it anymore.

"Who does this guy think he is?"

Mark was already involved in the hip-hop scene, and was practising at a local club with some friends. He asked me to come along, and I got to join in with them. I loved hanging out with Mark and his buddies; it increased my self-confidence as a teenager. Putting in some serious hard work, and a few bumps and bruises later, I was invited to try out with a new group that was forming. This guy already had a group, but they were all getting old, and he was looking for some new blood. Mark already knew most of them, so I decided to go along and try my luck.

After showing them my moves, they gave me the role of fill-in. They made the decision to go on tour in the summer, and as a warm-up, we performed at a well-known nightclub, and they asked me to fill in again, while the manager kept a close eye on me. No one spoke to me afterwards, so I didn't know if I had done good or bad, which left me feeling a little weird.

We performed at many different clubs all throughout the summer, and I became more regular with every show. We were asked to visit the southwest of England to promote our group, and I was chosen to go along. By this time I was improving rapidly, and was getting noticed. Our manager eventually bought a Volkswagen Camper van, and we used it to get around.

We were booked to perform at a graduation party in a large country estate, filled with middle-class students and people on the up and up. During our show someone had the audacity to throw a coin onto the floor, suggesting we were poor street kids dancing for money. I was enraged; who does this guy think he is? So coming out to perform some moves, I discreetly reached down to the floor and picked up the coin, launching it straight at him. The coin hit him in the face real hard, and that started the melee. The show ended promptly. We couldn't wait to get out of that place; well at least I couldn't, and didn't feel sorry for that guy at all.

"Hang out have a drink and relax"

No sooner did we arrive back in London, our manager called us into a meeting; I assumed we were in trouble. A big club had booked us for two weeks on the Isle of Man. I'd never heard of that place and had no idea where it was, but the prospect of travelling to it was exciting! We took a 4-hour drive up the ferry and departed from there. The crossing to Douglas, Isle of Man, took a few hours, but the excitement, made it fly by. Reaching the port of Douglas, the weather was dull and overcast, but it didn't take away from the fantastic colours strewn along the promenade. It had a backdrop dotted with hotels, restaurants, pubs, and B&B's all lined up alongside each other as if standing to attention for their daily inspection. The island even had a fully operational horse drawn tram service, built in 1876. I had never seen anything like it. We were met at the ferry port and driven to our hotel; the driver said he would meet up with us again later that day.

The club we were performing at was called The Lido, and it was massive! It was perched on top of a very steep hill and overlooked the whole beach. As we walked inside I struggled to take it all in; the foyer was massive; it was fully carpeted, and filled with all types of gaming machines on either side. As we passed the games, we saw a big arch on the right, and that was the entrance into the club area. It was enormous! My head swung around trying to take it all in, as we were immediately taken upstairs to the DJ's booth.

"You're on in five!"

It overlooked the massive dance floor below, which was positioned right in the centre of the club, balconies circled the entire top floor of the building and the club below. I would say it could take at least half an hour to walk around the entire building. Cocktail bars were strategically placed on every floor, giving those more reserved the option to hang out have a drink and relax.

He showed us the new sound system that had just been installed, with a full laser light show and smoke machine included; it was a great piece of kit. He then told us we'd be on twice in the evenings, 10pm and again at 11.30pm, with other groups performing before us. I had just turned sixteen, and our oldest member was eighteen so we were not that experienced with this kind of gig. Yes, we dropped in and out of clubs on a regular basis, but not a two-week private booking, that was new to us. Not to mention the very familiar and open atmosphere that went on backstage.

The women in our changing room sat topless chatting away as normal; I've never felt so embarrassed and tried not to gawk at them. We were on next and waited backstage. As the room door opened I took a gander outside and could see across the stage; the club was filling up fast. I grabbed Mark by his top and pulled him towards me, "Look at all the people!" I said excitedly. His eyes bulged as he took a quick swig of air; his response was minimal, "Wow!" We shook each other like two kids in a playground shouting, "We're doing this man! We're really doing this!" It was incredible and a little overwhelming at the same time, as the sound of the crowd roared backstage; the noise erupted loudly every time the stage door opened.

Suddenly a guy stuck his head inside and hollered, "You're on in five!" We finally made it to the big stage; this was our moment! The door opened, and we were ushered on as the group before us rushed offstage. The crowd had finished applauding, and were waiting silently to see what we were about to do. It was the islands first taste of break dancing, so there was a lot of expectation thrust upon us.

We lined up on the stage like deer's in headlights; I could feel my heart beating inside my chest. Then the music started, the sound was incredible, so crisp and clear, nothing like the other venues. We knew what we had to do and instinct took over, as the music carried us through the performance with ease. Filled with excitement and intrigue, we got to the end of our routine, and the crowd erupted into an ovation, it was astonishing to see such a response from a huge crowd like that; we were all blown away.

"My head was in a spin!"

After the show, we split up and went our ways to mingle with different people within the club. I spent most of my time walking around taking pics with the locals. I did get the strangest request from a guy though who asked, "Could you dance with my girlfriend? She's leaving for Ireland tonight." Not knowing what to do, I gladly obliged.

Man, that was surreal! At closing time, we met up and headed back to our B&B. That first night we all slept like babies; it must have been the long journey combined with all the excitement. The next afternoon, we all got up and went to check out the promenade, which had an assortment of shops and restaurants; we didn't know where to start. Mark and I went into a newsagent to get a drink and a bar of chocolate, when Mark politely said, "Morning."

The shopkeeper had a confused look on his face; pointing up to the clock on his wall; it was 4.30pm! Talk about embarrassing! I couldn't believe we slept in that late.

As we continued checking out the buildings, we came to a place called "The Hawaiian Bar" - a Hawaiian themed pub with flower neck garlands and beads hanging from the rafters. It had sliding doors next to the dance floor, which opened up, looking out onto the beach. It was pretty busy for an afternoon, so we decided to hang around and get some drinks in, to be honest, Mark was never a big drinker, but I was very keen.

The second night at the Lido was crazy packed, and the atmosphere was electric. That evening we were introduced to some interesting men and women, who were insistent we came to a casino named Whispers. I had no idea what to expect, and asked one of the bouncers I made friends with, a hardened Scouser from Toxteth. He told me it was just down the road, and he'd also be going there later, which reassured me.

"We were their private dancers"

At closing time, we met up with them, and they took us to the casino; the entrance was very posh looking, surrounded by glass mirrors, and big crystal chandeliers, which hung from the ceiling. As we got to the payment booth, our friends walked straight in, as did our older group members, but the doorman intercepted me; he looked me up and down and said, "Can I see some ID fella?" Confused and not knowing what to do, I had to think. He continued, "Are you a member of this establishment?" Before I had a chance to answer, one of the men we met earlier hastily led me away from the bouncer saying, "It's ok, I'll take care of this."

He took me over to a lady behind a glass screen and said, "Here, she'll take care of you," and walked off. My head was in a spin! What's going on? I just stood there. The lady behind the screen noticed the lost look on my face, and hastily handed me a small form, "Here you go darling, fill that in." Looking down at the boxes, name, address, age, etc., I swiftly filled it in, and handed it back to her. She picked up the form, took a little time to read it, then screwed it up and threw it in the trash. Now I was puzzled. She tilted forward glancing down through the arch in the glass saying, "You are eighteen aren't you?" Not knowing what to say I panicked, and then I thought to myself, wait! I never asked to be here; they invited me!

But before I finished my internal dialogue, she repeated it; this time with a different tone in her voice, "You are eighteen aren't you!" Then I understood... She wasn't asking, she was telling. Realising what was going on, I replied confidently, "Oh, yeah, of course," decisively nodding my head. She then handed me another form, which I promptly filled in, this time with my date of birth and the amended year. I was now old enough to be a member.

As we got inside, comfy maroon sofas and small round tables were dotted about with the odd semi-circular booth for people to chill on. Also at the back of the casino was a modestly sized dance floor, with steps leading up to an elevated platform with the DJ booth on the right. I headed straight for the bar and ordered myself some drinks. Being familiar with alcohol already, I thought it would be a good idea to experiment with other types of beers, cider and different kinds of spirits. Trying to pay for drinks was impossible for us, but I tried nonetheless, but the barmaid wouldn't budge; she may as well give me the keys to the city.

"There was no lasting damage"

An announcement rang through the speakers by the DJ, "Soul Sonic Rockers are in the building and are putting on a show for us." I couldn't believe what I was hearing, wait, this time of night? It's nearly 3am, are they serious? Seeing as they made provision for us to be in there, we felt obligated to perform. There was no way around it; we were their private dancers. More like performing monkeys! We bowled out of that place at about 5.30am. Later that afternoon I woke up with a colossal headache and felt sick.

Mark was already up, had breakfast, and even made his bed; He was always such a do-gooder. Getting myself together, I brushed my teeth, put on some clothes, and we were out the door. While walking along the promenade, I convinced Mark to come in the Hawaiian bar with me to get a liquid lunch, and chill out. While there, we got talking to a couple of Irish girls, Mary and Caroline.

They came over to sit with us, and we chatted for a while until they went for a boogie on the dance floor. It was time to leave, we had to be at the Lido to prepare for the evening, so one last drink, then we made our exit.

When the lido closed, Mark and I arranged to meet up with Mary and Caroline, to walk them home before we went on to Whispers. The journey to their place was captivating, old-fashioned street lamps arranged along the steep roads, that climbed and sloped into the hills and valleys.

A standard one-mile walk in this town felt like an eternity, but made for a cool evening stroll as we finally reached our destination. The evening was romantic; the moonlight shone down, giving us just enough light to see, while the street lamps complimented it by glistening in the distance.

"I was a little apprehensive"

The area was very rustic; there was an old cobblestone wall outside their hotel, with a black cast iron gate. Mark and Mary walked towards the front of the building, and I settled myself on the wall outside. Caroline stood directly in front of me as we continued our conversation.

We clowned around and giggled together like a couple of school kids, and it was nice; I hadn't felt that relaxed in a very long time. As we joked around her hand occasionally touched mine, which gave me tingles, eagerly anticipating the next contact. At that point, I wanted to kiss her, and as our eyes occasionally met, I got the sense she may want to also. The thought of rejection had continuously governed my mind during the night, and I was a bag of nerves. So with that said, I was never going to make the first move and kiss her.

Sensing my hesitation, she moved in and took the initiative. But she leant in towards me right at the time I looked down at my shoes, Boom! I head-butted her in the mouth. I couldn't believe that just happened. Thank goodness there was no lasting damage, and I still got to kiss her; I think she deserved a kiss after that. Mark and I agreed to meet them again at the Hawaiian Bar the next day and said goodbye. As we hiked down the hill replaying our final moments with the girls, it made the trip back to Whispers fly past.

When we got inside whispers, the casino was in full swing; people jammed the elevated dance floor, boogying to the latest 80's pop hits, while others sat at tables quietly conversing over a glass of wine or beer. Still excited from my earlier moment with Caroline, I went straight to the bar to order some drinks. While sat there talking to the barmaid, a particular waitress named Liz was returning some empties, and pinched the back of my neck. Looking around inquisitively at her, she just smiled and walked away.

I thought she was affectionate like a kind of big sister thing, but this continued a few times. Mark and the others laughed when I told them about it. One of them said, "Martin, don't be silly, she'd never be interested in a little boy like you," while walking away shaking his head chuckling to himself.

Again, that same old feeling of frustration and rejection flooded my mind, which then turned into resentment. As a consequence, I ended up battling with anger too, which came from not dealing with those feelings. After all, I was a little apprehensive about that grown woman, who was showing an unhealthy interest in me.

"My head was all over the place"

The next afternoon, we met up with the girls and were having a great time on the promenade. I was still on my liquid lunches, which thankfully didn't seem to bother Caroline too much. The time we spent together was invaluable to me on so many levels; this island was a free for all, people flocking to bars and clubs looking to get hooked up with someone to give them an interesting story to tell, or to put another notch on their bedpost. I was never interested in that, for me this was unpolluted and natural.

I wasn't looking for sex; my last sexual experience was only a few years earlier aged twelve, while drinking with a neighbour across the road from mums; She plied me with red wine and took my virginity, then in a moment of sheer insanity, took her own life. It was hard to process that dreadful situation, and I was still trying to put it behind me.

So the lure of permitted sex wasn't that exhilarating, as far as I was concerned, but rather assurance and stability. I was finally discovering it with this sweet Irish girl.

We concluded our evening with a nice romantic walk on the beach, and then eventually back to their hotel. We made our way to Whispers and found the guys gathered around a table discussing our wages; not wanting to miss that, I quickly sat down and paid attention. Without thinking, I brazenly picked up someone's drink and necked it down, placing the glass back on the table and hastily wiping the excess from my mouth.

"She frantically put her hands over my mouth"

It was then I noticed Liz sitting directly opposite us, she was with her boyfriend and some friends; she waved her hand in my direction gesturing me to come over. I looked behind me, assuming she may be calling someone else, but no, she was calling me; the guys were speechless and looked bewildered. I tentatively got out of my seat and walked towards her, slowly sitting down next to her. As I did, she started being overly affectionate to me, stroking my hair and kissing me on the side of my face.

It was good to see the guys' jaws dropping, but I didn't feel comfortable at all. As she kissed me, her friends looked on in shock. At the same time her boyfriend slammed his drink down and stormed off; I was dumbstruck. She then turned to me and said sternly, "Martin, I want to see you at closing time - I need to speak to you." Not knowing what to do, I just said, "Ok, sure," and got up from the table to sit back with the guys. I stared into space as the lads grabbed my shoulders and shook me yelling "Yes, Martin yes!" My head was all over the place.

Closing time had come, and I was well and truly plastered. Completely forgetting about what happened earlier, I was ready to head home. Suddenly Liz appeared out of nowhere and swiftly closed the distance, separating me from the guys; I was caught completely by surprise. Sensing my nerviness, she stroked my hair out of my face saying, "Are you afraid of me Martin?" Trying not to show fear, with a sober look on my face I promptly responded, "No, I'm fine!"

She then took a firm hold of my hand, and led me straight out of the building. It was well into the early hours, and I had no idea where she was taking me. I assumed she wanted to talk, but she led me away and had a tight hold of my hand, tugging me along the road not saying a word. As I glanced at her, she had a determined look on her face, as if she had an intended destination in mind.

We finally ended up on the beach, and it was there she suddenly switched. Stopping me in my tracks, and turning towards me, she grabbed my face with both hands and said, "Martin, I want you desperately." I just froze! Breathing heavily, she began to kiss me very passionately and sometimes uncontrollably while biting my mouth and neck multiple times! I tried to get into it, thinking that would somehow make it better, but I couldn't get rid of the uncomfortable feeling in the pit of my stomach. I was desperate to get away. So, while she continued to bite my neck, I looked around for someone or something to distract us.

"I couldn't have felt worse"

Before I could get my focus, she stopped abruptly, grabbed my face with both hands and looked deep into my eyes. Licking her lips and taking a deep breath, she sighed and said, "Martin, let's go back to your B&B." I was stuck and didn't know what to do. I took a deep breath and told her straight, "Listen Liz! I can't do this; I just can't." She didn't take it too well, and became hysterical begging me. Feeling the tension I grabbed her by the arms and said firmly, "Look Liz, I'm not doing this, I'm just not!!"

Right at that point, one of my friends came walking past us along the road. I deliberately called out to him, as she frantically put her hands over my mouth, trying to stop me as I resisted her. Sensing her time was well and truly up, she finally conceded. With a look of disappointment on her face she said, "Fine, if that's how you want it, I'll see you later," and walked away. Man, I was relieved.

When I got back to the B&B it was practically morning; Mark was flat out asleep, so I quietly climbed into bed and tried to nod off. Waking up, I'd forgotten most of last night and was in the middle of freshening up, when I got the shock of my life. Love bites all over my neck! It was disgusting! Mark was annoyed, and as far as he was concerned this was just typical of me; another stupid act on my part, possibly jeopardising our chances with the girls. Because they were best friends, Mark thought it could ruin his relationship with Mary.

We were meeting them soon, and I had no way to cover it up, so I wore a polo neck jumper; it was so obvious wearing that on a hot day. We got to the Hawaiian bar, and I ordered my usual, but this time a large one, Mark then took Mary straight to the dance floor. To make things worse, Caroline looked gorgeous and was being affectionate with me. I mean, this was everything I ever wanted, right here within my grasp. Desperation hit me, and I felt utterly dreadful and decided to bite the bullet, and tell her what happened. Honesty is the best policy. Well, at least that's what I heard.

While sat there, I was trying my best to pluck up the courage to tell her about it. But, before I had a chance to open my mouth, she clocked something was wrong. And in one fluid movement, she leant forward and pulled my collar down. I sat as still as could be, as she stared at the love bites on my neck; she was visibly upset. Expecting a rollicking, I readied myself to take a hit, and then if lucky, a makeup kiss, But no. She just sat back into her chair and said casually, "Well, that's ok, it doesn't matter, I mean, after all, it's got nothing to do with me." I thought that was a strange reaction and her comments confused me.

"Despair hit me like a tidal wave"

I looked at her for a few seconds, trying to understand what she meant, but nothing was coming back. So I responded, "Well that's ok then." She then shrugged her shoulders and said, "Fine," and those were our last words to each other. I was so confused and played it over in my mind. I figured she liked me and sincerely cared. I concluded she apparently didn't care, and was ok with that.

My heart couldn't have been more crushed! I had lost the one girl I cared about because of a crazy situation that was out of my control. Not knowing what to do, I decided to get over the whole mess by indiscriminately putting myself about, acting like I didn't care, when in fact I did. I hooked up with all kinds of girls, attempting to have fun when the truth was... I couldn't have felt worse. I dreaded going back to Whispers that night knowing that Liz was there, but what else was I to do. After all, she destroyed my only serious relationship, which meant I had nothing else to lose.

I got inside, and the club was at full capacity, so hoping to go unnoticed, I headed straight to the bar for a drink. I chatted with the barmaid and we were having a stimulating conversation, when suddenly her expression changed and her eyes dropped to the floor. Turning around on my bar stool, I noticed Liz standing a few feet away from us, with a look of fury on her face, that's when I saw her boyfriend too, heading in my direction. Oh man; here we go, it's kicking off. Quickly swigging the last few drops of my drink, I hastily got off my stool and kept the glass in my hand just in case.

Getting closer, he walked right past me, waving his finger saying, "You! Follow me." I thought to myself, Ok, I get it, he wants to do it outside. Putting my glass down and giving the worried barmaid a reassuring nod, I marched towards the exit. He stood there on the spot, and as I approached, he didn't move an inch. I found that a little unpredictable and it threw me off. When I reached him, I was transported right back to my childhood. He came straight at me, grabbing my collar and pulling it down.

"My emotional breakdown was perfectly aligned"

It was like mum scrubbing me behind the ears as a kid. Looking at my neck, he just sighed and said, "Liz did that to you didn't she?" It was the strangest scenario, my adrenaline was pumping ready for a fight, but now my dad was questioning me. I just stood there nodding obediently, "Yeah, it was her." He then clued me up. "Listen, mate, don't kid yourself, you're not the only one, she'll soon forget about you, and it'll be someone else next summer."

I tried to explain to him that it was completely one sided, but he stopped me in my tracks, "It's ok, I don't blame you, whenever we're having problems this always happens." Feeling sorry for him, I had to ask, "But why would you stay with someone knowing they'll do that to you?" He just smiled, put his arm around me and said supportively, "Come on kid, let's get back inside before the bar closes." Sitting on my stool and knocking back a glass of scotch, I was still thinking about that unanswered question...

why would you stay with someone knowing they'll do that to you? It troubled me. I gazed out into the club, and observed the look on people's faces, they seemed happy enough, smiling away as they danced and laughed, without a care in the world.

Then it came to me, a sudden realisation; it's all a front! These people are here because they have nothing better in life. These clubs are where they come to forget, where dreams come to die, and all hope is dashed. People trying to evade the painful truth of their wasted lives, using sex mixed with copious amounts of alcohol as their only means of escape.

Mum warned me about this place as a child; it's called the knackers yard, when you've got nothing left, that's the place you go. An enormous surge of despair hit me like a tidal wave, and I fell into an instant depression. I had been taken for a ride this whole time, and the people I thought were honest were not. It was all a big charade.

"Don't you bring those girls up here!"

What an idiot! That was the moment my convictions changed. There was to be no wedding, no wife, no white picket fence, it was all a lie, and my emotional breakdown was perfectly aligned. The island was at record capacity that month with people pouring in from all over the UK and Ireland. It was in all the newspapers and on every TV; people were flocking into the Isle of Man from everywhere, and I was going to make the most of it!

My only strategy at that point was to live in the moment and get smashed out of my head doing it. My relationship with Mark was hanging by a thread; he was still with Mary, and probably still annoyed at me for nearly screwing everything up for them both. Our two-week contract was nearly up, so they booked us for another four weeks because of the high demand on the island.

I couldn't believe my luck! They checked us into a huge hotel further down the road, with balconies overlooking the beach; it was a complete contrast to the other B&B. As usual, Mark and I roomed together while the other guys did their own thing. Seeing as we had another month on the island, you would think I'd pace myself, but no. I wasted no time and spent the next few weeks regularly getting drunk. On one of our nights off, I was up late getting leathered. It was around 2am and Mark was in bed trying to sleep. I stood outside on the balcony in my underwear, erratically yelling at the crowds as they rolled out of the nearby clubs. While standing there making a fool of myself, two girls looked up and recognised me; we exchanged pleasantries for a while then one of them shouted, "Hey, do you think we could come up to your room?" I was delighted!

Mark stuck his head out from under his covers with a gruff voice, "Don't you bring those girls up here, I'm sleeping!" Ignoring his warning, I muttered to myself, "Shut up you old fart, and go back to sleep." Then quickly shouted our room number while waving the girls up. Mark grumbled while turning over and pulling the covers over his head; he didn't appreciate my antics. The girls and I joked around for most of the night, drinking and frolicking in the huge bedroom. We climbed into bed together and eventually passed out.

"My usual mix of beer and spirits"

The next morning I woke up, the girls were gone, and I had a colossal headache. Jumping out of bed, I went to see if they were in the bathroom, and even checked Marks bed too, but there was no sign of them. Looking on the floor, I realised my clothes were missing too. Maybe I put them in the wash? I reassured myself, but after checking, they weren't there either. Suddenly I had this bad feeling. I rushed over to my wardrobe and yanked the doors open...

They took all my clothes! I rushed back towards my bedside table and checked the draws... Oh no! They had taken my wallet too, and all my money was in there. Those girls had stolen everything I had. I was furious! Being so incensed, I got into a state of bitterness and anger, which then led to more drunken outbursts and embarrassing situations.

I had become the statistic, no hope, no dreams and trying to mask it all with alcohol and sex. It seemed like no time at all, that the island started to empty. The clubs rapidly became a shadow of what they had been, and even the casino was dead. We had been living in a bubble for these few precious weeks, not realising people had real lives to get back to now the summer of fun was over. The place looked like an empty shell, and it was quite depressing.

We were moved out of the hotel, which they probably couldn't afford anymore, and they stuck us in a house that was vacant in the area. It was a struggle for us all to be honest, as we tried to recreate those moments we had when the place was buzzing, but those times were never coming back. The evenings were pretty dull, and the attendance at the club was abysmal; however, I didn't mind, because I'd soon be at Whispers getting drunk.

It was a ghost town! Even the DJ's music didn't improve the atmosphere; it was eerie. They no longer needed the drink order sheets so, while sitting alone doodling on the back of one of them, I got talking to a local model named Jenny; she lived and worked on the island and was easy-going, also very polite for someone so beautiful.

"I was happy to isolate myself"

Noticing my drawing she asked, "Martin, would you draw one of those for me?" Replying kindly, I said, "Sure, what would you like me to draw for you?" Her response surprised me. "Draw me a picture of you!" I thought that was kind of interesting so I replied, "Ok then, a picture of me it is," and drew a caricature of myself as she patiently observed; then handed it to her.

She looked at it and smiled to herself. Right at that moment all the guys came rushing over to our table and started laughing, but I didn't feel like being sociable. So, getting up and making my exit, I headed straight to my usual spot at the bar to speak to my friendly barmaid. Serving me my usual mix of beer and spirits she asked me, "You ok Martin? You seem a little down."

I took the metal tray loaded with alcohol in my hands and said while walking away, "Yeah I'm fine, I'll be ok in a minute," sitting myself down at a single table. Trying to silence the negative thoughts that plagued my mind, I guzzled down one drink after another until I was well sedated. Suddenly I heard, "Come on Martin, get up there and show him how it's done," in the distance; I looked up and could barely focus. Some of the group were goading me, but seeing as I was completely out of my nut, I didn't understand what was going on. Apparently, there was a guy in a cabaret group on the island who drew himself a small crowd.

He got up on the stage to rap and even started break dancing too. The guys wanted me to show him how it's done, and boasted to the people around them how good I was. "Go on! Get up there!" They shouted at the top of their voices, but I could hardly focus, and my head was a mess.

Eventually getting to my feet and wobbling over to the stage, I climbed the few steps up to the dance floor. The room was spinning, and I could hear the guys in the distance saying, "Watch this! Watch what he does!" Taking a deep breath, I gazed at the floor, and the crowd went silent... Crash! Slumping to the ground, I collapsed.

It wasn't long before someone helped me off the dance floor. What a humiliating experience. I'm sure the guys were embarrassed too. I felt so angry inside, because it wasn't my idea to get up there in the first place. If that wasn't bad enough, as an encore, I gave everyone the middle finger as I left the stage, to the disgust of many. They carried me back to my seat, and that's where I fell into a deep sleep.

"The privilege of sleeping next to her"

The next day, that incident was thrown in my face many times, and I wasn't allowed to live it down. That was my cut off from the rest of the group, and I was happy to isolate myself. Jenny invited everyone to her house, and I wanted to go, but not with this lot, I just couldn't take being singled out anymore. So I walked off towards our house while everyone else went with her.

To my surprise, while walking away, I heard her voice behind me, "Martin where are you going?" Without turning around, I shouted, "Home to watch TV." She rapidly responded, "You can't go, I need you to come round to my house, it's important." Now that was intriguing; what could she possibly want with me? So turning back I went to investigate. We got to her place, and the guys took up the sofa and chairs while giggling and being noisy, as Jenny disappeared into her bedroom.

I was sat there with the guys when suddenly Jenny reappeared out of her bedroom, "Martin could you come in here please, I need you for a sec?" I was in shock! The guys were all looking at each other and must have been thinking, wait, not this again! So, I sheepishly got up and walked into her bedroom. As I entered the room, she pulled the sheet off her bed and spread it out neatly on the bedroom floor. She then reached into her jeans pocket and pulled out a piece of paper. It was the cartoon I sketched for her the other night. She then said, "I want you to draw me a full size picture of you on this sheet." Feeling honoured, I didn't know what to say. She then said, "I want to keep this to remember you by." She had the paints and everything in front of me, so I couldn't say no.

"Time to grow up and move on"

Starting with the outline, I got to work. She left the room to entertain the guys. By the time I finished, it was late, so she invited us to stay over. I had the privilege of sleeping next to her in bed; it was all very innocent. We got up early that morning which was a first for me, and we ate breakfast together, my first alcohol-free one. That was a first for me too. Jenny took us for a walk into town and to be honest; it was one of my best days on the island.

I was used to the bustling summer crowds always bothering us for photos etc. but this was different, just the usual locals chilling out while shopping. It felt good to see the normal side of the island. While in town Jenny said she had to shoot off, she quickly gave me a big hug, kissed me on the cheek then disappeared. I never saw or heard from her again.

I made the most of my last two nights on the island, and it was great. The morning we were leaving, we all stood at the ferry port with our bags, wondering where all the time had gone. We weren't happy going back to reality, but that's life. Some of us were starting to show signs of wear and tear, especially me. It was probably time to grow up and move on, and that's what we did. The break dance machine had finally given out, and we officially retired. We were no more.

CHAPTER 4

LOVE, MADNESS AND JESUS

Although the break dancing adventure was well and truly over, I still found it hard to let go of my other destructive habit... drinking. My brother had moved on, so it was easy for me to do whatever I wanted, without worrying about anyone or anything. I never put the Whispers days to rest, and spent most of my time talking about them instead of putting them behind me.

I had been away for what felt like a lifetime, so it was good to catch up with some friends from the neighbourhood. Like me, they also enjoyed a good drink, so we swigged ourselves into obliviousness, Scotch whisky, Thunderbird, Tennent's Extra Strong and Special Brew lager, we had it all. We listened to music, talked about life, and I occasionally danced a little; never being able to regulate my alcohol consumption, I'd often drink into the next day. We met at a friend's house, went up to the local flats and set up the ghetto blaster.

Hanging out and drinking was a consistent routine, as there was nothing better to do. Plus, my friends always wanted me to repeat the dance routines I did on the island, and it kept the memories alive. It was good having something to keep my mind occupied, as the travelling came to such an abrupt end; this helped me get it out of my system gradually. Leaving that kind of life behind and trying to get back to some normality was a hard transition for me. The truth is; I self-medicated whenever I found myself in a position I couldn't or didn't want to deal with, and that was my real problem.

My friends and I got a little too smashed one evening, and as usual, I ended up unconscious. I eventually woke up about 1.30am flat on my back, in a random front garden. It was raining heavily, and I wasn't wearing a shirt, and my trainers were missing too. I was soaked! Word had it I got beaten up and mugged for my shirt and trainers; somehow I didn't believe that story. Staggering to my feet,

I sluggishly walked home as the rain beat down on me. When I eventually got to my house about thirty minutes later, I went straight upstairs, slipped off my jeans and climbed into bed.

Laying there trying to relax was tough; I had a mammoth headache, and ended up vomiting all over myself. My stomach was empty and I suddenly felt drained. I was too fatigued to clean up the mess, and quickly drifted into unconsciousness. The endless pattern of drinking and vomiting continued for quite a while, until the opportunity I had waited for, finally came.

"Score some gear"

Mark came round to see me and had this look on his face, like a father hiding a present behind his back for his child. He said, "Are you still interested in training?" I responded, "Yes! Why?" He continued, "There is a new gym just opened down the road, do you want to join it?" My head bobbed up and down throughout the whole conversation. He then said, "You will have to listen to everything I tell you, and do as your told. If we are going to do this, we're going to do it properly."

I couldn't care less, I wanted this so bad, and expressed it zealously, "Mark, where do I sign up?" I couldn't contain my excitement; I was finally going to start weight training at last! Drinking large amounts of alcohol had suppressed my appetite, and I was looking scrawny and pale. But that was all about to change.

Walking to the gym was intense! I was going to get my first real experience of bodybuilding up close, and couldn't wait. Finally getting inside the gym, I was so excited that I couldn't wait to get started. The gym was in an old warehouse building, so it was open plan. The walls were all whitewashed and covered in mirrors.

There were lots of fancy machines I had never seen before. Mark started me off gently with the little weights, until I gradually got the hang of it. Wanting to give me the best chance of getting fit and healthy, Mark instructed me on what supplements to take, and how and when to take them. They were ok for a while, but I needed something stronger. After getting to know some people, I managed to score some gear (steroids).

If there was one thing I learnt about my life, it was this: I worked well with routine, but if left to my own devices, I would go off track. But right now, my life was finally starting to make sense. I had to make changes regarding income. I rinsed all my show money on alcohol, and now needed a steady income, to pay for all the supplements I took for training. It was time for a steady job.

It wasn't long before I found one at a local sweet factory. My sister Susan worked there too, so I had company. It was an excellent job, and I enjoyed it. My ability to work on initiative served me well, and scored me many brownie points at work. When it came to training, I was extremely disciplined, and that became my new form of self-medication, this time with anabolic steroids.

Diligence was an understatement for my new way of life, as it was strict and regimented. There was no time for messing around or going out; I went to work, the gym, then straight home for my dinner and off to bed. Mum and I were getting on well at this time, as I was giving her rent regularly, then storing the rest of my money in a pot in the living room.

"I knew it could wreck my whole life routine"

Being meticulous in the gym, at home, and at work, helped me gain lots of muscle, which gave me a healthier look, and made me feel good too. I was also attracting more attention from the ladies, which boosted my confidence. The summer was sweltering, so I decided to have my lunch out in the yard, and that's when I noticed this girl standing outside the admin building. Figuring she was new, I walked over to say hello. She told me her name was Carol; she moved down here from up north and was hoping to get a job. I stayed for a brief chat then went back to work. I didn't see her again that day and assumed she hadn't got the job.

I did see her again a couple of days later, but this time in uniform; she was working on the basement floor. My job required me to move around the factory floors quite a lot, which meant I saw her regularly, while passing through her department, we shared an occasional glance and smile. At some point, I figured we would have to speak to each other formally, or at least I was hoping to. We finally spoke one day when I was looking for my union rep and went to find him in his favourite tearoom. As I entered, she was sitting there alone and I was caught completely off-guard. I was so nervous and almost began to stutter, but thankfully she put me out of my misery, inviting me to sit down and have a cuppa with her.

Naturally I accepted, and we had a good chat. She was stunning, and I knew it could wreck my whole life routine, but…she was lovely! Looking back, I know it wasn't the best idea, but that's how you learn - from mistakes. I saw her from time to time, and it always made me feel gooey inside. At lunchtime, I would check to see where she was sitting in the canteen and then make my entrance. I'd act all surprised when I saw her, and then go about my business. I'm sure she never realised what I was up to, but always seemed happy to see me.

It was the final day before the summer holidays, and I found out some guy in the factory wanted to ask her out, and there was no way I could sit back and let that happen. So, I dashed to the canteen and seeing her sitting there made my move, "Hey Carol, how are you?" She gave me an inviting smile, and we quickly got talking.

I noticed the other guy coming to speak with her, so I went for it. "Carol, would you like me to walk you home after work?" Without hesitation, she answered promptly, "Yes, that would be great, I'll meet you outside after work," hearing that, the poor bloke looked dejected and walked away. I couldn't contain my excitement! I pulled myself together and was ready to meet her after work.

During the afternoon, I got held back and was worried that she'd be gone, it was at least half an hour later than usual so, l conceded that she'd probably left by now. When I finally came out, the yard was like a ghost town, and it couldn't have been anymore deflating. Walking towards the exit gates, I noticed a figure in the distance, but couldn't be sure it was her. But it was! She was still waiting.

While walking her home, I asked if she wanted to come out to a club that evening (my friends were hiring it out for the night) and she said yes. I was chuffed. Finally reaching her road, we agreed to meet there at 7:30pm. It was around this time John came into my life, six foot two with a real menacing look.

I don't specifically remember how we became friends; it just evolved. He was a man of the world, very clued up with a strong sense of loyalty, unlike any other friendship I'd had before. The defining quality about him was territorial; John didn't like anyone to mess about with his friends.

I came home from work and was buzzing; John was there with mum having a cuppa and a chat. I told him about my hot new date, and he was super excited for me. "Come on you," he exclaimed, "We're going to get you fitted out," dragging me out the door and down the high road. He took me into some clothes shops and helped me pick an outfit for the evening. After I had bought some new threads, it was time to get home and get showered. I arranged to meet John at the nightclub later.

"I heard screaming coming from her room"

Going to meet Carol I went through a stack of emotions, playing out scenarios in my head of what to say and how to respond, I was so nervous. As I waited at the bottom of her road, there was no sign of her; it was now nearly 8pm. I thought Carol was going to stand me up, but was relieved to see her in the distance coming down the road. She looked gorgeous and was enthusiastic about the evening.

We got to the club, and all my friends were checking her out. I never had a full-time girlfriend up to this point, so they were all curious to see what my choice was like. We had a great time doing the rounds, showing her off to friends, downing a few drinks and having a dance. It was now time for some privacy, so we sat on some stairs near the exit, and that's where we had our first kiss. It was incredible, and I was love-struck for sure, hoping she felt the same.

We eventually went back into the club, and spent the rest of the night socialising. I asked her if she wanted to stay with me that night, and she agreed, so we headed back to my place. After being on my own for so long, it was a nice surprise waking up next to someone; it was a pleasant change. Saturdays were great; my uncle Tony frequented our home, always looking for things to do. He and mum were spending the day in Southend, and asked if we wanted to come too! For me, it was the perfect follow up from yesterday, and we made the most of it, hanging out on the beach and finishing up in a pub. Carol stayed over again, but went home on Sunday, and we caught up at work Monday. Several weeks later, and mum was back in Italy. Now I had a girlfriend, my house was always full; it was the strangest situation.

I know some of the guys probably liked her and that was reasonable, as she was beautiful. My friend Darren was involved with a girl named Helen around the same time; cute and super easy to get along with; she had a young daughter from a previous relationship. She was living in sheltered accommodation at a local hostel, and we hung out there often.

"I'm going to kill you"

One evening, while heading over to the hostel to catch up with Darren, I saw him leaving the building from a distance with his brother-in-law Gary. As they rushed off, I heard screaming coming from her room, so hurrying upstairs to see what was going on, I quickly reached her door. Rushing inside, I found her crouched on her knees with her head in her lap, she was crying while rocking back and forth.

I could see that she was clutching her hand and appeared in great pain, so kneeling down beside her, I tried to get her attention and calm her down. Managing to prize her hands apart I could see one of them was severely damaged. Something had happened between her and Darren, and in a fit of fury and an act of self-flagellation, she grabbed a bat and smashed her hand with it. Trying to understand what happened, I promptly called an ambulance and sat with her as she slowly opened up, telling me the story.

"Well, Darren turned up as usual, but this time with his brother in law, he was acting very strange and a little distant. It was just after I challenged him on his behaviour, that he became angry and without hesitation, dumped me in front of his brother. So assuming it must have been my fault, I took my little bat and smashed my hand with it."

After hearing that, I felt sorry for her and a little guilty too. The truth is, I spoke to Darren many times about his actions; he always did this... When he got bored with girls, he would just finish it with them and move on. The first time I met Helen I could see the way she looked at him, she loved him indefinitely. I figured it might all end in tears, but hoped this time would be different, but not so. The ambulance finally arrived and took her to the hospital.

He needed to explain himself, so I hastily left the hostel and went to find him. I located him at the top of the road where he lived, sitting on a wall with Gary. I was so furious; I had played the situation over in my mind so many times, that when I reached him, I was visibly enraged. I shouted at him, "What happened between you and Helen?" But before he could answer, Gary butted in, "What's it got to do with you?" Getting right up in his face, I said sternly "Mind your f***ing business; you'd do well to keep your mouth shut."

To my surprise, he unexpectedly kicked me in the chest, sending me reeling backwards into the road, while jumping off the wall. I couldn't believe it and thought to myself, did he just do that? He started to freak out, shouting loudly, "I'm going to kill you, you're a f***ing dead man!" I just stood there thinking, wow, he is mad! He ripped his t-shirt off and stood there flexing at me; after all, he was pretty muscular. He did a good job working up into a state, then abruptly charged towards me, waving his arms aggressively.

"He looked a sorry sight"

Adrenaline rushed through my system as I waited for my moment, resigned to the fact one of us was going to get hurt. I dipped my head; kept my eyes on the target and threw a right cross with bad intentions. Crack!! It landed clean and caught him smack in the nose and mouth. There was silence and no counter punch. As I briefly looked up, he was stood there with a glazed look on his face; his head dropped to the side, and in one continuous motion, he fell slowly back toward to the ground like a felled tree.

His head cracked against the solid concrete, as his lifeless body bounced across the floor. It was a horrible sight. Yes, I wanted to defend myself, and yes, I was angry and a little nervous, but didn't want to hurt Gary like that. After all, it was Darren I was annoyed with, not him. I hurried over to see if he was ok, and Darren rapidly dived in front of me, trying to stop me from finishing him off. We grappled as I sought to explain myself.

82

The neighbours heard the commotion and came rushing out of their homes. Seeing Gary lying in the road with his face covered in blood, one of them crouched down to get a closer look saying inquisitively, "Man, what did you hit him with?" That comment made me anxious; I honestly thought he was dead. Up to that point, I had never hit anyone with such bad intentions as I did at that moment.

The gully quickly filled with blood, as it trickled liberally from his face and head; he was still completely unconscious. I took off my jacket and carefully lifted his head, placing it underneath waiting for him to come around; it was nerve racking and took about twenty minutes. I just kept thinking to myself, why does this always happen?

He started to come around, and my face lit up as he slowly began to open his eyes. As they came into focus, he saw me, and the look on his face changed! Still concussed, He pushed me to one side as he swiftly got to his feet and darted off into the distance.

Darren was still hurling verbal abuse at me, which was getting us nowhere, so it was time to go back and check on Helen. When I got to her place, her hand was in a bandage, but she was settled. Luckily she had no broken bones, just badly bruised. While we were talking, I figured it best not to mention what just happened, and spent most of the night cheering her up, talking into the wee early hours until we both fell asleep.

"It will all end in tears"

I woke up a few hours later and decided to go straight to work; Helen was still out cold, so I tucked her in, and silently made my exit. When I got into work, I told Carol I was at my mum's that night, but someone had beaten me to it. Right out of the blue Carol said, "Does the Louisiana hostel mean anything to you? How did she know about that?

It came to my knowledge that Darren's older brother told her, (he fancied her and was hoping to score some brownie points). I explained to her what happened and kept to the truth - I couldn't lie to her. Thankfully she believed me, and that was the end of it.

The thought of what happened to Gary the other night wouldn't leave me, it left me wondering what happened to him after he ran. Where did he go, what did he do? That's when I made the decision to squash the beef with him, and headed to his house. His mother answered the door and went straight into a rage, "What are you doing here? You're in big trouble you know, I'm calling the police right now!" I Quickly reassured her, I was there to apologise and nothing else; she then managed to calm down.

Gary appeared from behind the door, and his face was a mess, his nose and mouth were badly damaged, and he looked a sorry sight. "Gary mate, how long have I known you?" I said supportively. "You know I'd never do anything like that don't you?" Looking down at the floor he agreed, "Yeah I know, it just got out of hand, but you caught me with a good shot though." He said while laughing. Even his mum managed to see the lighter side of it all; especially when she realised I wasn't there for trouble.

"A warning sign for me"

Finally putting that fire out, I had the task of making it up to Carol. Mark wasn't around much, and with all these distractions going on, I eventually stopped going to the gym altogether. My efforts to please Carol had tipped the scales too far, which created an unhealthy dependence on her, causing me to unravel mentally. It even got to the point that I couldn't work, and found it hard being away from her. The truth is: I wasn't sure if I was falling in love or going insane. All I know is this: at that moment nothing else mattered to me.

We both ended up leaving our jobs, and she temporarily moved in with me. Mum took an instant dislike to her and didn't mind letting me know, "It will all end in tears," she'd say regularly. Up to that point, I had been getting on with mum very well, so maybe I should have taken her advice, but decided to ignore it instead. Things got out of hand at the house between Carol and mum, so she decided to move in with one of her family members who lived near by.

When she moved out, my relationship with mum quickly began to collapse, and we barely spoke. She hated Carol so much that she made up all kinds of stories about her to get me angry, and it worked. There is no way I could stay in the house listening to that garbage, and figured it was a good time to leave. Carol and I moved from place to place, and it got pretty tough at times, and left an open door for paranoia to set in. It was hard trying to shake off the stories mum told me, and they steadily chipped away at my mind.

Things got worse when Carol received a card, and a rose from an old boyfriend; she had the audacity to give him my address to send it to her. I was furious, but Carol seemed to find it amusing, and that angered me all the more. She even patronised me while we were arguing in the street, so I pulled off one of her shoes and threw it over a garden fence. I told her, "Go get it b***h," then stormed off.

My emotions were all over the place. I thought to myself, what am I doing here? How did I get in this state? Things were all good until this happened. My mind was up and down like a yo-yo, perfect one minute and sad the next. That's when my temper started to change. I went back to see where she was, and found her wandering the streets. Wasting no time, I quickly apologised, and we made up. But that should have been a warning sign for me.

She eventually got a job in a superstore and was promoted soon after. I was so proud of her progressing so quickly, and always knew she had it in her. I picked her up at the end of each day and had to endure blokes occasionally trying to chat her up while I was waiting. It never bothered me though, as I knew at the end of the day, she was coming home with me. But as she made new friends, and went to parties with them, that certainly changed things.

"Paranoia, mixed with insecurity"

Feeling vulnerable and a little left out, I started spending time with my old sparring partner Gary and began binge drinking again. Whenever Carol went out, Gary and I hung out at his aunt's place; she liked a tipple too. On one particular evening, we all got a little inebriated, and I wasn't able to go home, so we had to stay over.

Things got out of hand with his aunt and me, which left me feeling terrible. I never stayed out all night, so Carol was naturally anxious. So that next afternoon, I arranged to meet her for lunch at Appleby's, a small diner, opposite her workplace.

Wanting to surprise her, I arrived a little early and got us a good table in the middle of the restaurant. When Carol walked in, I smiled at her, but she looked kind of sad.

She sat down and started to speak about stuff, I could feel her sadness and reached out to take her hand, but as I did, she silently burst into tears, "I missed you last night Martin, I had no idea where you were, and thought you were with someone else." Watching her break down swiftly racked me with guilt and shame; it broke my heart. Keeping a tight hold of her hand from across the table, I reassured her that everything was ok. I decided to get a job at the same store, in the hope it could help our plagued relationship.

I applied for a job, and because of her influence; I got a quick start. Although the position I got presented a problem; it meant differing shift patterns for us both; Carol finished work when I started and vice-versa. I didn't like the idea of that, but she seemed ok with it. Paranoia mixed with insecurity, meant there was a good chance I could lose this job, and it wasn't long before that happened. After getting into it pretty bad with my supervisor, he said he had no choice but to let me go.

"I got panicky when it became dark"

Carol didn't take the news very well, and no matter how much I tried to explain, she just didn't want to know. I could feel the distance between us, and it was getting me down. This situation was the start of our relational decline, causing regular heated arguments. Emotionally, I was in a horrible place and felt as though I couldn't do anything right, when out of nowhere; it came to an abrupt head.

Right in the middle of a blazing row, I started losing control and bang! Something had broken in my head, and without warning, an overwhelming tidal wave of fear crashed over my body, sending me into an intense panic. I don't know what happened or where it came from, but it was the most horrific thing I have ever experienced.

Cutting the argument short, I ran out of the house gasping for air, my heart was beating hard like a freight train, and I thought I was going to die. Running around the streets and disappearing into the night, it felt like a heart attack as I stopped occasionally, trying to figure out what was happening to me. I eventually found myself near Darren's house, so I decided to knock and see whether he was there. His older brother Paul answered and could sense something was wrong, so he invited me in and made some tea. Darren was out at that point, which left us on our own.

As I opened up about what happened, he started speaking to me about the Bible and this Jesus character. Religion never interested me, but I wasn't about to argue, I needed the help, so I decided to shut up and listen. The talk did give me a level of comfort but to be honest, I didn't understand any of it

The anxiety went on for some time, and I found it hard to work, as I was constantly on edge. Struggling to sleep in the evening caused me to stay up all night, so I slept during the day instead. I got panicky when it became dark, and only relaxed when it was daytime. My doctor put me on anti-depressants, which only seemed to exacerbate things.

Carol and I were barely spending time together, as she worked during the day when I slept and was tired from work when I'd be wide-awake. I did everything I could to keep myself calm, but it was pointless as nothing helped me; I had to concentrate on something to keep my mind occupied. Carol always asked me what was going on, but the embarrassment was too much for me, I figured she'd think I was an idiot.

My mental health caused us a lot of problems, and it put a massive strain on our relationship. I tried to make things better between us by meeting her for lunch, but being wasted through a lack of sleep made it futile. My irregular sleeping patterns were starting to get up her nose, but there was nothing I could do; after all, I didn't even understand what was going on with me!

CHAPTER 5

STOLEN CARS & BROKEN HEARTS

My old mate Gary was staying up late at his parents' house, ringing premium rate numbers, and clocking up bills over £200. The situation was perfect for me; he liked staying up at night; and so did I. We stayed up looking at motor magazines; he loved cars and knew loads about them. Stalking the streets in the early hours, we looked at cars in the area. Mum had a friend from East London who regularly borrowed me hers. I didn't even have a driving license.

While out driving around and having a laugh, Gary noticed a Ford Escort RS2000 and asked me to stop while he had a look at it. He got out and walked around the car. He then came back over to me and said; "Meet me at the traffic lights at the top of the road in ten minutes." I didn't know what he was up to, but did as he said. I got to the top of the hill and parked up at the lights. There was no sign of him, so I decided to head over to his house to see where he was.

Suddenly out of nowhere, I saw blinding lights coming towards me, and then heard a loud screech! I looked over to my right, and it was Gary; He had a big smile on his face. He somehow managed to disable the car alarm, got in and drove it away. Giving me the thumbs up, he took off from the lights and quickly disappeared into the distance. We met at his mum's house, had a look over the car, and it was gorgeous!

"She needed a break from the madness"

We had fun driving it through the streets of London till the early hours, and then hid it in a local housing estate. Later that day, we went to pick it up, but to our surprise, it was completely stripped. It would now have to be replaced. So Gary and I went on a car theft spree that lasted a few weeks. I had several cars lined up outside my home, and drove them all regularly. I quickly got a reputation, and was named The Driver; after evading a police car and Sherpa van at the same time. They chased me around our area and I managed to give them both the slip. That news quickly got around. To make an impression on Carol, I asked if I could take her to work in one of my cars, and she reluctantly agreed. Gary followed in his vehicle, and we ended up racing to her workplace.

I took a detour through some garages to beat Gary to it, but he actually got ahead of me, and took the same short cut I had in mind. He had stopped up ahead, waiting for me to catch up, and as I came flying around the corner at high-speed, I had no time to think, and smashed into the back of him, totalling my car. The front was completely caved in, and Carol and I were both trapped inside – Gary had to pull us out through the passenger window.

Thankfully, Carol wasn't hurt, and I was more embarrassed than anything else. We finally got her to work safely in Gary's car, but she wasn't happy at all, and I couldn't blame her. After all, why would she be happy with me? I was wasting my life nicking cars, while she worked a job and paid the rent. It was a no-brainer.

My old pal Peter was living in a squat near me, so I paid him an early morning visit. He eventually opened the door, and wiped the sleep away from his eyes, saying, "What's going on man, what you up to?" Smiling from ear to ear, I answered, "I thought I'd come check on you, you know, see how you are." Walking away from the door, he mumbled, "Well, this is me." I followed him into the squat, and tried to grab his diminishing attention, while explaining to him what Gary and I were up to. I now had his attention.

He didn't have a run-around and needed to get about; so I gave him one of the cars to help him. We had a daily routine; at around 5am I'd pick him up, and we'd go for some breakfast, then a drive into the country somewhere; we did that nearly every morning. Carol decided she needed a break from the madness, and took a trip up to Newcastle to spend time with family.

When she got back, we got on better than ever, and I was starting to fall in love with her all over again. That inspired me to treat Carol to a couple's night out, with Gary and his new girlfriend. I wanted to take them out in style, so I pulled out a Ford Granada 2.8 Ghia X. We drove all through Essex enjoying the night lights and stopping off for a quick drink, before dropping off Gary and his girl, then heading back to Carol's. But the fun wasn't about to last, as my extracurricular activities were about to catch up with me.

It all happened around 5am while Gary and I were racing around the streets. My car suddenly conked out, and I made a quick pit stop to get it fixed. Opening the bonnet, I noticed the battery had broken free from its holder and had fallen into the engine. Gary decided to go for a walk while I got busy trying to fix it; dawn was breaking, and it was getting light.

"They dragged me out the car"

Tinkering under the bonnet trying to repair the problem, I suddenly became aware of vehicles approaching, so I peaked over the lid, and noticed three police cars and a van. Trying to be discreet, I put my head back under the hood and carried on working. Some time had passed since I'd last seen Gary, and I wondered where he was.

The police pulled in, and two officers came over to me asking, "Do you need any assistance?" Taking a deep breath, I answered politely, "No officers, but thanks for asking." The dialogue went on for a while, and they kept asking me all sorts of questions, "Is this car yours? Do you have proof of ID? When did you get the vehicle?" I remained calm throughout, and made sure I answered their questions confidently. The police bought it, and that was my opportunity to get out of there. I was free.

Just as I was getting into the car, the policeman said, "Hold on one minute sir." What now! I climbed back out of the car, only to see two officers holding Gary in handcuffs. "Do you know this man?" One officer asked. Thinking quickly I answered, "Nah, not personally, but I've seen him around." The officer turned away and said, "Ok, you can go," while walking back to his car.

To my surprise, Gary shouted, "Yeah, that's him!" Before I could do anything, they dragged me out the car and slammed me onto the ground; slapping handcuffs on me. I was furious! Not only had Gary grassed me up, but the police roughed me up too. They picked me up by my arms while they were behind my back; I thought my shoulder blades were going to pop out of their sockets. The police were thrilled with their catch, and boasted about what they would do to me back at the station. We were detained at a local police station, and kept in separate cells for questioning. Stints in those cells felt like an eternity, you had no concept of time, and you could easily get disorientated in those small rooms.

While being interviewed, they informed me Gary had told them everything they needed to know, the cars outside my house and Peter too. I couldn't believe what I was hearing; Peter had nothing to do with any of this. Then it came to me; Gary bought himself a lighter sentence at the name of his accomplices. The only problem is, Peter wasn't one of them.

When they brought Peter into the station, I could hear the anger in his voice as it echoed through the building, declaring what he was going to do to Gary when he got his hands on him. Gary was soon released but dug himself a huge hole. The police kept me in longer, trying to gather more evidence, which was frustrating, but I was used to it.

"He had been laid into pretty bad"

You see, I was around when the Sus Law was in full effect. It permitted police to stop and search you, and potentially arrest you if they felt you were suspicious enough. I lost count the number of times I was stopped and detained in a cell for hours, just because I was hanging out in the wrong place or with the wrong person. So I was well familiar with it.

Minutes felt like hours in that isolated cell, until they finally let me out for more questioning. While sitting through another salvo of pointless questions, they finally gave in and took me back to my cell. On the way there, I noticed Gary being booked in again. He was re-arrested trying to steal another car. What a Muppet!

That made me feel a lot better, and I'm sure Peter also. After what seemed like a lifetime, Peter and I were finally allowed to share a cell. We spoke all night about what had happened, and Peter was cursing his bad luck, as he had nothing to do with any of this. I reassured him that I made that entirely clear in my statement. When we were finally released, we walked out of the cells into the waiting area, and Carol was sitting there. Man, was she a sight for sore eyes! Grabbing her hands I asked, "How did you know I was here?" She said, "I got worried when you didn't come home two evenings in a row, so I rang Gary's mum, and she told me what happened. So I came straight away."

Waiting to be sentenced was a very worrying time; I didn't want to go to prison. Carol and I were a lot closer now, so I promised her my driving days were well and truly over. We got to the Magistrates' Court, and there was no sign of Gary; they detained him until the trial, he was a liability. When Gary finally made it onto the stand, they placed him next to me, and away from Peter; who was still incensed by what he had done.

Gary looked rough; he had been laid into pretty bad and had a black eye. As he lined up next to me, Peter leant behind me and whispered softly toward him, "You're a f***ing dead man!" Nudging Peter back in line, I felt a little sorry for Gary; he was in enough trouble already without having Peter on his case.

"The greatest amount of humility"

The judge came in, and it was time for sentencing. "Gary, please stand up. I am charging you with three counts of TDA (taking and driving away), no insurance and no driver's license, how do you plead?" He answered: "Guilty." The judge paused and said, "I am sentencing you to four months in prison." He was then led away.

"Peter, please stand up. I am charging you with no insurance, no driver's license, TDA and receiving stolen property. How do you plead?" He answered, "Guilty." The judge then said, "You will pay £50 for no insurance, £50 for no driving licence, £50 for TDA, £50 for receiving stolen goods and £50 for court costs. I am also giving you a year's driving ban." He then stood down.

"Martin, get up." The judge then started his sentence. I didn't hear anything at that moment, I just glanced back at the public gallery watching Carol cry; it broke my heart. I didn't want to be away from her right now. The judge said, "I seriously considered a custodial sentence for you Martin, as it is evident to me that you are the ringleader." I thought that couldn't be good, considering the penalty dished out to Gary. The judge continued, "However, as it is your first offence, I will order that you pay £250 damages and costs, a year's driving ban and a year's probation." He finished his sentence with, "I sincerely hope I never see you in this court again, do you understand me?" With the greatest amount of humility I answered, "Yes your honour." To be honest, I would have paid a million pounds at that point! This whole situation put a lot of strain on Carol, and it left me feeling incredibly guilty.

"We could sense something was wrong"

Going straight was easy enough, but suffering from severe stress and anxiety wasn't helping my situation. There is nothing worse than watching your life flushing down the crapper, knowing there's nothing you can do about it. I always felt demoralised, and that helped my decision to leave Carol for her own good; it was going to be one of the toughest choices I ever made.

She made something of herself, a good job, excellent prospects, and was pretty and talented. I however, seemed to be the opposite on every level. On the surface I seemed stable, but my mind was a muddle of confusion and suspicion. I was never good at talking about my feelings, and that had a lot to do with my upbringing. "Stand up straight! Look at me when I am speaking to you! Don't cry or I'll give you something to cry about." It didn't exactly nurture the feeling of safety while opening up.

No sooner had I decided to go straight, trouble found me. There was a bug going around, and I was feeling very ill. Peter popped in to cheer me up, and said enthusiastically, "One of my mates owes me some money, and he just gave me £50, come on, let's go out, it's on me." I felt weak and maybe should have stayed in, but I was being offered a free night out, how could I resist? So, throwing on some clothes and grabbing my trainers, we left.

The West End was our usual haunt, so that's where we headed. Peter dragged me into the Moulin Rouge Cinema to watch a dirty flick, but there was a problem. Peter handed the money to the cashier, and he immediately held it up to the light to check the note. I sensed something was wrong. The clerk argued with Peter, and we finally decided to leave. Peter got frustrated and said, "Forget that place man, we'll go somewhere else instead." Keeping our eyes peeled for another fun place to hang out, we strolled into Shaftesbury Avenue. That place was always bustling; it had an array of fast food joints, with the odd local artist sketching caricatures for the hordes of keen tourists. As we casually walked along the avenue, when the Vice Squad came out of nowhere and pounced on us; I was slammed to the floor, while Peter was pressed up against a concrete pillar. They cuffed us, swiftly loaded us into separate cars, and sped off.

We were detained at a local police station and held for quite a while. The police treated forgery very seriously, and interrogated me for most of the night. But after another session of prolonged questioning, I was finally locked up with Peter; he looked rough and seemed a little out of sorts. I felt quite drowsy myself, and we were sure that they had given us both downers, hoping we might grass on each other.

Peter told me what happened, "The police took me back to my squat looking for more forged notes, but realising there weren't any, they brought me back. They weren't sure how to get back to the station, so I took them the long way around through Alexandra Palace. It was fun.

"That got my alarm bells ringing"

We were made to serve our time, and after gathering all they needed, they let us go in the early hours of the morning. Having no money to get home, we had to walk at least ten miles; we didn't mind though, we were just glad to be free. Then I realised, we'd be up in front of that same judge; the last time I saw him, he was adamant he didn't want to see my face again.

The court date was set, and I took the opportunity to speak to my probation officer and get her thoughts. She wasn't impressed at all, but promised to write me a good report. Peter and I were up in front of the Magistrates again, and were both charged with intent to use counterfeit notes and given fines. I only escaped going to prison because my probation officer wrote an excellent report. Even though I was grateful to be out, Carol finally had enough. I only wanted the best for her, but knew there was only one way to make her happy, I had to get out of her life. I got straight to the point, and told her we'd have to finish for the best. Her reaction surprised me; she collapsed to the floor in tears, asking me over and over, "Why are you leaving me, why?" Man, it killed me seeing her so broken, I felt so sorry for her, but had to remind myself why I was there. This was for her good, not mine.

She unexpectedly grabbed my leg and begged me not to go. That was it! Thinking of all the things I had put her through and how she stuck with me, I just couldn't go through with it. That night Carol and I were the most intimate we had ever been, and I knew that I would never feel the same way about anyone again.

Things went well for a week or so, and we seemed to be ticking along just fine. However, there was something I just couldn't put my finger on, which made me feel uneasy. When I met Carol this particular lunchtime it was different; people were distant, and there was an eerie silence in the canteen. It was strange considering I knew everyone in that store. I had worked there, and picked Carol up every night, but it didn't stop the uncomfortable feeling in the room. Seeing as my mental state wasn't the healthiest, I tried not to think about it too much, and put it down to paranoia.

Carol was getting up earlier for work now, but didn't want me to walk her to the bus stop. Again, putting it down to over sensitivity, I pushed it to the back of my mind. But the warning sign for me was our next lunch date, as I walked into the store, she engaged me in conversation while slowly walking me back out of the building, and then continued the convo outside. Maybe she thought I hadn't noticed, but I did. That got my alarm bells ringing, and I was now certain something was wrong.

"Thoughts of isolation and rejection"

Slowly getting my head together, I was now ready to get back to work. I told Carol the news about a recent application I made at a nearby factory, and she seemed happy for me. She said she'd be going out that night to a pub with work colleagues, and would see me later. It didn't bother me at first, so I decided to make myself scarce for a few hours, then meet up with her later. I didn't take my keys with me, assuming she'd be home around the same time as me.

I went to hang out with my friend Colin for the evening, and we had a good laugh. It was pretty late, so I made my way home before Carol went to bed. When I arrived at the house, the door was still locked and she wasn't there; it was very late and knowing the pubs were closed, I got worried thinking something may have happened.

I was outside for ages, and was now concerned. I considered going back to Colin's, and was just about to walk away, when I saw Carol coming up the road towards me. I asked her if she was ok, then asked her where she had been, but she was put out by my questions. She was cold towards me, and I got a sense there was something seriously wrong.

Once inside, we got into a massive argument, and Carol turned aggressive. No matter what I said, she found the bad in it, and so I went with my heart and asked her, "Are you seeing someone else?" Well, she caught me completely off guard with her answer, "Yes, I am!" I just froze.

"A harsh and valuable lesson"

I didn't know what to say. She continued, "I want you out by next Friday." Lost for words, and feeling physically sick at the thought of another man being with her, I felt confused. My emotions were all over the place, and I couldn't sleep. Strangely enough, Carol slept like a baby, and got up early for work as usual. I followed her to the bus stop, and someone picked her up in a car. I didn't know what to do.

So, I marched to her workplace, and saw her outside with her colleagues waiting to go in. I tried to talk to her, but she squirmed as I begged her to reconsider, "Carol, please don't do this, let's talk about it." She was having none of it, "Martin, you're embarrassing me, stop it." She said awkwardly looking around at the crowd. I even reached out to touch her, but she pulled away, I'd never seen her so cold. It was like she never knew me.

The stress, confusion and finality of it all brought me to tears, as thoughts of isolation and rejection gripped my mind. Uncomfortable at my public show of affection, she kept looking at the doors desperately waiting for them to open, and they finally did. Reaching for her arm, while trying to get her attention I said, "Carol hold on!" But she pulled her arm away and turned to me, "Listen Martin, I'm not interested, just get lost and go away!" She rushed into the store and didn't look back. None of this made sense. When I tried to leave her, she begged me to stay, and I promptly reconsidered. Oh, but now the tables have turned, and the shoe is on the other foot; she couldn't care less. And that taught me a harsh and valuable lesson.

"You're gonna have to leave"

People stared at me as I passed them on the street, tears streaming down my face as the heavens opened up. It was now raining heavily. The only light in all of this was the letter I received later that day, letting me know I got the job. I was starting on Monday morning, so surely Carol would be happy to hear that news. She may even re-evaluate her decision.

I went to meet Carol at her workplace, and it was surreal. People who usually greeted me avoided eye contact, and Carol resisted taking me upstairs to the canteen. She was different from this morning, much calmer and super friendly, but I wasn't buying any of it. I played along as she politely chatted away while walking me back to the exit, and it became apparent, the person she was seeing had to work in the same building. That's when I told her, "Listen to me Carol, I know your new man works here, but if you don't tell me who it is, I'll go upstairs and find out for myself."

Knowing I wasn't kidding, she hastily gave in and told me. "It's the Grocery manager." Pushing past her, I said, "That'll do me," and hurried back into the store as Carol chased after me. "Martin, please don't start any trouble, please, I'm begging you!" Heading straight for a worker in his department, I asked sternly, "Oi mate, where's your manager?" This cocky little runt (probably his best friend) answered, "He's not here, why?" Pausing for a second, realising he was never going to rat on his boss, I didn't waste my time. So I said calmly, "That's cool; I'll see you again soon."

Carol came clean, and told me she had been seeing this guy the whole time, even when I was meeting her for lunch; that's why it was so quiet in the canteen. What's even worse is this; everyone in the store knew about it, which explained why people avoided me.

The whole time, I blamed myself for being paranoid and obsessive. By the end of the week, I had moved my stuff back to mums. I dreaded going anywhere near that place, but had nowhere else to go. Grabbing the last of my things, and having a quick chat with Carol she interjected, "You're gonna have to leave, Matthew will be round soon." I felt so sick that I couldn't even look at her. I just left.

Moving back into mums came with four square meals of "I told you so" a day. My relationship with her was at its worst; she just wouldn't let it go, but constantly told me how right she was. When she eventually left for Italy, I couldn't be happier, finally some peace.

"He was deliberate and unnerving"

I was starting to give up on life, but my old pal John was there to help me through; He had been with me throughout the relationship and was very close to us both. He was seeing an Irish girl that was pregnant by him. They were having problems, and she had thrown him out too; we were as bad as each other. I couldn't leave him homeless and agreed to let him move in with me, at least until mum got back.

He did his best to get me out the house, taking me to a local nightclub and man it was fun; one thing is for sure, you were always guaranteed an enjoyable time with him. We stood at the bar drinking and talking while checking out the talent in the club, and that's when something caught my eye. I couldn't believe it! Carol was sitting only metres away with her new boyfriend and his entourage. Now, John had a soft spot for Carol, but only because she was with me.

So, trying my best not to draw attention to her, I engaged John in conversation, but it was futile. John and I were like two peas in a pod, he was never going to fall for that old trick and immediately realised something was up. He flared his nostrils, "What's going on Mart?" And started scanning the room; as he did, I closed my eyes, please don't let him see her, please don't. But it was too late; he spotted her and went into crazy mode. John wasn't wild and loud; he was deliberate and unnerving.

His face was now scowling as he said firmly, "Who the f*** do they think they are? Coming here with Carol right in front of your face." Before I could grab his arm, he was already marching towards them, and stood about six feet away, staring at them with his nostrils flaring. Carol's face said it all, she knew what John was about, and her new boyfriend seemed even more concerned when he noticed the look on her face.

Not knowing what to do, they sat there confused as Carol gave me a worrying nod, which was mental code for; please get him away from here. I went over and patted John on the chest saying, "Hey come on now, it's all good mate, come on leave it," while waving my arm in apology to Carol and her entourage.

"Live together, die together"

John never cared too much about what other people thought, but acted on impulse. That was all he knew; he was looking out for his friend, and I felt flattered. Although John was streetwise and well connected, he did have his own intense idea of friendship. Live together die together. Back at home; we sat up till the early hours drinking. He encouraged me to get over carol while promising me a good time. The only problem with that was, you just never knew what he meant by a good time.

He brought two girls back to my place after a night out, waking me up with all the noise. I went downstairs and asked him, "Hey John, what's going on?" One of the girls interrupted, "Why don't you just go back to bed; you're ruining our fun." John put his hand over his eyes, knowing I wouldn't put up with that nonsense, and he was right.

I quickly responded, "Shut your mouth b***h and get out of my house... now!" She was a gobby cow and started giving me a load of verbal, "Yeah well, why don't you just f**k off and mind your own business." John intervened and quickly pushed them out the door.

I explained to him that although we were good friends, he shouldn't take the mick; he got the hint. I figured John might be happier if his girlfriend moved in with us, seeing as she was now heavily pregnant. After running it by him, he thought it was a brilliant idea and went to tell her. They eventually moved in, and when I finally met her, I wondered how they got together; she was so easy-going and incredibly sweet, and he was... well, you know... a lunatic. It wasn't long before he was up to his old tricks again though. This time he brought another girl into the house, while his pregnant girlfriend was upstairs sleeping; and again, he thought it was no big deal.

"Into a corner against my will"

We got into a heated argument, which woke his girlfriend, and I could hear her coming downstairs, so I hastily escorted the girl out the front door and into the street. I think John's girl knew what had happened, as I'm sure she'd probably been through this with him before. An argument then broke out between them, and I made myself scarce, heading to bed.

During the night, I woke up to the sound of raised voices coming from the kitchen beneath me, and I was sure my name got mentioned. I lay there for a while waiting for them to calm down, and managed to drift back to sleep. Startled and abruptly woken by the sound of screaming, I jumped out of bed as quickly as I could, and ran down to the kitchen. The scene was alarming; John had one hand around his girlfriend's neck pushing her up against the cupboards, and a large kitchen knife in his other hand held against her stomach; he was threatening to kill her and the baby.

I had to think fast! We got along pretty well, but I'd never seen him like this. So approaching with caution, I said, "John, put the knife down," but he wasn't interested! With his eyes locked on her, he said sternly, "Stay out of it." I knew then, I was going to have to turn up the heat, "John, bro, I'm not joking, I suggest you put it down now!" But he was having none of it.

It was scary; I knew he was capable of this sort of thing, but not with his girlfriend or me. It had now developed into an unpredictable situation. She had her eyes closed and was in great distress, obviously fearing for her life. These were the same conditions I experienced as a child, having violence forced upon me, which never felt good. Fearing for his girlfriend, while trying to deflect the attention off her, I made my move.

100

Grabbing his arm and redirecting the blade away from her, he turned it on me. He sliced my wrist as we grappled around the kitchen; I yelled at her to get out, while trying to get the knife from him. We struggled back and forth as blood splattered the cupboards and floor, until I eventually got on top of him.

I finally had the knife, and was able to take a breath. The thought of getting stabbed for no reason infuriated me, and I lost it. Seeing the blood from my wrist sent me into a fit of rage; I took the knife and pressed it hard up against his face, "Is this what you want, eh? I swear, if you do that again, I'll take your f***ing eye out!"

He said nothing, but just stared at me coldly. I think after what just happened, he wouldn't have cared if I killed him. That's when I became aware of his girlfriend crying, "Stop, please don't do it, please!" Seeing that look of shock on her face stopped me in my tracks; I made my point. John grabbed his stuff and left that night; she pressed charges and had him arrested, and he went to prison.

That moment in the kitchen had taken me back to a place I hadn't been in ages; it left me feeling vulnerable, muddled and irritated. Plagued with feelings of frustration, I couldn't explain why my life was in such a mess; I felt unable to get past it. When John tried to stab me, it was a reminder of the cruelty of life, and that's what I had to endure.

"I considered doing something unthinkable"

Being forced into a corner against my will, brought up feelings I thought I had got past. But the truth is, that episode opened a door to more insecurity and then anger. Because of that, I talked myself into confronting the man who ruined my life, by taking my girl. My friends at work told me it was a bad idea, and that I shouldn't go, but I couldn't help myself.

During lunchtime, I went to Carol's work to get this sorted once and for all. On arrival at the store, Carol noticed me entering and came straight over to confront me. "Martin, what are you doing here?" I answered casually, "I am here to see Matthew," she begged me not to say anything and tried walking me to the exit door. I wasn't having any of it this time, and went straight to his department; the same little upstart as last time greeted me. I didn't pull any punches this time though, "Get Matthew!" I said sternly, he tried to reply with the same pre-programmed response: "He's not here." So, I swiftly interjected, "Listen, he's the manager, he has to be here every day, now turn yourself around and go get him, because if you don't, I will!"

"A desperately sorrowful expression"

He then looked at Carol, and the expression on her face let him know I was deadly serious, so off he went. It wasn't long before Matthew came down and cautiously strolled towards me. Before I could say a word, he held his hands out in front saying, "Look, no problems mate." I stood there thinking, No problems? Are you having a laugh? I got straight to it; "I want to talk to you over here!" Walking away from Carol towards the wine aisle, in the corner of the store. She had a concerned look on her face as we walked away. If only he knew what was going through my mind, he would have never followed me there.

We reached the wine aisle, and again he instantly started to talk. I held my hand up to his face and stopped him. "Do you know what you've done?" I said coldly. He seemed very uncomfortable and apprehensive, "Listen, mate, I don't want any trouble with you, It's something that just happened." It was at that point while staring into Matthews' face I felt myself increasingly losing control; the weight of the situation had begun to consume me as I considered doing something unthinkable.

Waiting for my moment, I looked down at my feet and took a deep breath, ready to move. Looking back up, I caught a glimpse of Carol behind him in the distance, and as my eyes focused, it was a strange sight. She was standing there like a mannequin with a desperately sorrowful expression on her face.

All of a sudden it hit me, this is what they all think of me, this is what she wants them to see, Martin the loony. I then knew the only closure I would get, is proving them all wrong. I can't tell you how the anger subsided, but it just did. Calmly and consciously I said, "Carol is very special, just look after her and treat her right." I shook his hand and walked off.

As I paced towards the door, Carol stood there crying, I walked over to her and pinched her chin, "It's ok Carol, it's over now," and left silently. I finally had closure. About three months had passed, and I was beginning to put it all behind me.

I was busy with my duties at work, when one of my colleagues said there was someone outside to see me. I couldn't think who it might be, but went to investigate. Pushing the button to open the shutter, I watched it disappear upward. I got the surprise of my life; it was Carol!

"This is it...I'll see you"

I didn't know what to do or say; I was in shock. She stood there crying, "Matthew dumped me, I don't know what to do, I'm so sorry about what happened between us, Martin, trust me I am." It had to be one of the strangest and most exhilarating moments of my life. My head was saying, tell her to sling her hook, but my heart wanted to comfort her. She asked me softly, "Look, I understand if you don't want to, but do you think we could get together later and talk?"

Trying my best to be cool, I answered, "Maybe, I suppose we could go out for a pizza when I finish work, how's that sound?" She smiled and said, "That would be lovely, I look forward to it." She stood there smiling. So grinning back I said to her, "I'll see you." She slowly turned away and answered, "Yeah, I'll see you." While walking into the distance, occasionally looking back.

We went out that night, and Carol suggested we go back to her place to eat our pizza. So we did. While eating, she started telling me things I didn't want to hear, like how much better in bed I was than her ex. But to be honest, it made me feel sick; the thought of her with someone else was already enough to make me gag. So I just tried to sift through it.

When we finished eating, I got up to leave, and she suddenly asked, "Why don't you stay here tonight? It's getting late, I really don't mind." My head was a mess! I hoped this wouldn't happen, but at the same time wished it would. I knew staying over wasn't the best idea, but we agreed; she'll keep her bed, and I'll take the floor, and that's what we did.

During the night she called to me, "Martin this is stupid, why don't you just get in here?" It was late, and I was half asleep, so it seemed harmless enough. We were intimate that night, and it was incredible.

In the morning, we sat down for breakfast and Carol was smiling from ear to ear, "Why are you smiling? I asked inquisitively. Still grinning she answered, "I suppose its contentment." We were almost back where we started, and that troubled me a little.

Later in the day, we went out to do some shopping and were very close. It was genuinely nice, but without warning the strangest thing happened. The day was coming to an end, and she was buying something at a chemist, when something came over me. She was standing at the counter waiting, and I put my hands on her shoulders and gently spun her around. I then kissed her. She looked up at me curiously, and it came out, "Carol, this is it... I'll see you."

We both knew in our hearts, this moment was right. I walked out of that chemist and out of her life. The last thing I remember was looking back through the window, and seeing her standing there with a big smile on her face. That night we spent together was the closing chapter of our lives.

CHAPTER 6

JESUS IN THE DARKEST PLACE

My doorbell rang, and I slowly got up to answer; I fractured both my heels in a fall, and was resting. Finally opening the door, I couldn't believe what I was seeing - it was John! Inviting him inside, he filled me in on what he had been up to in prison. He had his jaw wired because someone broke it, no surprise there. He told me he had been working while inside, and had plenty of money to spend.

He suggested we buy some threads, and then get our friends together for a reunion. So I hobbled along with him to get some new clothes, and then we went for something to eat. After we had spent hours looking at clothes, we moved on to McDonald's. John ordered enough food to feed an army, so we sat upstairs with all the families. John was busy stuffing his face with burgers and chips, while telling me about his prison experience. When all of a sudden, he stopped the chatter and said, "Wait a minute!"

He stuck his fingers into his mouth, scraped around the edges of his teeth, and pulled out a big lump of chewed-up food. He held it on his finger, then let it rip, sending it flying across the restaurant and sticking onto a nearby window. I was nearly sick. He found it hilariously funny, and we quickly made our exit. He always felt that I was a killjoy, because I didn't find things like that funny; it just wasn't my style. He begged me to get hold of Peter so we could go out again, just like we did in the old days, so I called Peter, and we all got together.

As usual, we were back at our old haunt, the nightclub on the high road; and it was going to be an exciting night. When we got there, we bumped into a friend of Peter's called Brian from the old neighbourhood. We all agreed to get together and finish the night off. It was terrific being back at that club, and we were having a great time. All of a sudden, one of Peter's friends came over shouting: "Brian is outside, there's a problem." Peter went outside to see what was going on, and eventually came back to get John and me. Brian got into an argument with a guy in the club and was head-butted in the face, nearly breaking his nose. In an act of retribution, he smashed a glass and stuck it in the guy's head. When the doormen saw the commotion, they seized hold of Brian, gave him a good hiding, and then flung him out.

"We scrapped under the moonlit sky"

So after hearing the news, we decided to wait for these guys to come out. They eventually did, and there were at least fifteen of them, and only the four of us. Completely outnumbered, John thought that was excellent odds. One of the guys came over to us and said, "Do you lads want to have it?" Under the circumstances, and with these odds, none of us thought it was wise, and remained quiet.

Although, I did take a mental note, seriously hoping I'd get the chance to take him up on his offer another time. You see, anyone can give it when with loads of friends, but when they're on their own, that's a different story. Those guys eventually left, and we all felt a little humiliated. We saw a friend who was working as a cab driver, so we all jumped into his cab and set off. Brian invited us back to his place to hang out.

As we were driving through some back roads in the local area, we were all in deep conversation about the upcoming shindig at Brian's. When suddenly, someone shouted, "Guys look!" We gazed out the cab window, and passed a group of men walking along the road who had noticed us looking at them, and stopped in their tracks. "It's them; it's them!" Brian shouted at the top of his voice, jumping up and down in his seat with excitement, while randomly slapping each of us.

John yelled, "Hey driver, stop here please." But I quickly grabbed the drivers' shoulder and said "No! Go a little further down the road and then stop," we don't want to give the game away. The driver continued a few yards further, but his cab doors were already flying open, as this lot couldn't wait to get out. He screeched to a halt, and we exited the cab. We acted as casual as possible, trying not to draw attention to ourselves. There were five of them standing on the corner of the road talking, pretending not to notice us. But as we got a little closer, we recognised them. It was the smart mouthed guy that glassed Brian with four of his pals. They had seen us drive past, and were now wondering what to do. As we approached, to our surprise, the biggest guy bolted the minute he realised who we were. Those mental notes come in handy, you see, I was about to tick mine off.

Only a couple of yards away from them, we exchanged a few words, but I was having none of it. With that earlier humiliation still fresh in my mind, I didn't want to waste time with worthless dialogue, and punched the first guy to get us kicked off. We quickly separated into different directions, as the others picked their targets. Punches and kicks rained down as we scrapped under the moonlit sky, but the fighting didn't last long.

"Such a mindless and vicious way"

The guys knew they were beaten and scrammed. Brian & Peter appeared from across the road laughing, "You alright Mart?" Brian asked. Dusting myself down I answered, "Yeah I'm good bruv," I looked around and noticed John was missing. Fearing something may have happened to him, I asked the guys, "Have you seen John?" Looking around, Peter answered, "Nah, we lost him in the melee."

It was right at that moment, we heard the sound of screaming coming from around the corner. We dashed around there as fast as we could to see what was going on. By the time we arrived, the screaming had stopped; there was no one around, and it was surprisingly quiet. We couldn't find John, but came across a semi-conscious guy lying in a doorway; his face was splattered with blood.

We glanced over the road, and saw John running towards him. He passed us at blistering speed and pulled his foot back, and I turned away. Just the sound of his shoe smashing into this guys face was enough for me. It was the most horrific thing I had ever heard. The guy couldn't even get his arms up to defend himself, and we didn't have a chance to stop him. Still in shock, I grabbed John and herded him into the cab, as we sped away into the darkness. John was angry with me, because I got annoyed with him, and we argued all the way to Brian's about what he had done.

We nearly got into it ourselves. Brian managed to calm the situation, and as the adrenaline wore off, we all simmered down. I know what I did wasn't right, but what he did was way beyond reasonable. We fought guys who fought back, and they were able to defend themselves. But kicking someone in such a mindless and vicious way was well over the top. We eventually got over it and managed to put it behind us.

There was talk about us having a party for a while, and after what just happened, we all felt it would help clear our heads. So that morning, we put the word out and arranged it at Brian's flat, later that evening. I was looking forward to it. I spent that morning lazing around, and saving my energy for the upcoming do.

"The game was up"

John came bursting into my room and said, "Martin get up, we've got a wedding reception to go to." I couldn't remember him mentioning it before. So clearing my eyes, I asked, "Really? Who arranged that?" He responded casually, "Yeah, a friend of mine invited us, and I forgot it was today. Come on, get ready, we'll go straight to Brian's from there." I decided to get freshened up.

We were both dressed up and heading to the wedding reception. Arriving at the venue and entering the hall, I immediately noticed that all the people were Asian. It did make me a little apprehensive at first, but when John walked straight in and mingled with the guests it eased any fears. The hall was majestic, fully fashioned for the wedding party, with pearl coloured drapes hanging from the walls, with a gloriously large fully lit chandelier centrepiece.

I grabbed myself some food, and even had a drink with some of the guests. Standing in the foyer with a group of people, a lady casually asked, "So, who are you friends with, the bride or groom?" Not realising what was happening I responded confidently, "Actually neither, I'm friends with John, he was the one invited."

Some of them had concerned looks on their faces. "Who's John?" One asked. I then turned and scanned the reception room, trying to locate him. And there he was, dancing with a lady with a drink in his hand. "There you go," I said confidently pointing right at him,

"That's John, the one dancing with that lady." By the looks on their faces, I could tell something was wrong. One of them headed straight for the bride and grooms table. I didn't need to figure out what was going on; John had done it again.

I didn't even wait for the bloke to reach the table, thinking quickly, I excused myself and asked for directions to the bathroom. Someone kindly pointed it out to me, and I hastily made my way there. Heading to the hallway, John spotted me and quickly realised the game was up, so as the guests were trying to locate us both, John and I met in the foyer and quickly made our exit.

Once we were at a safe distance, I grabbed hold of John and said, "I knew I shouldn't have agreed to go anywhere with you." He just laughed. That's all he ever did in the face of shame or adversity... laugh. John was a chancer, He had no invite, and didn't even know anyone there, he just took it as another opportunity to get free drink and food, before the real party began; to his credit, he was good at it.

"I know I could have killed him"

When we left that wedding fiasco, we were both pretty inebriated and headed to the party. When we got there, it was packed! There were so many people we didn't know, and it was great - I got rid of John for a while, which gave me some space. It allowed me to talk to some other people in the hallway. As usual with me, I ended up on the door.

There was a guy who lived on the estate, who was pretty well known, and had a bit of a reputation. So while letting him in, I hadn't noticed John come out of the kitchen, and was stood in the hallway behind me. This guy acknowledged everyone he passed, until he got to John, and then something changed. As soon as they set eyes on each other, there was an instant and mutual dislike.

As the guy looked at him, John said, "Can I do something for you?" And it all went south from there. As the chap attempted to respond, John head-butted him in the face, and they went straight at it. You couldn't swing a cat in that hallway, so I decided they would have to take this outside. I grabbed the two of them and thrust them towards the front door, but unlucky for John, his foot caught the step, and he fell onto his back. The other guy instantly started kicking him as he tried to get back to his feet. I couldn't watch that happen to a friend of mine and eventually managed to stop them. They agreed to go their separate ways, and we all finally started to enjoy ourselves again.

During the evening I had quite a lot to drink, and think it may have been spiked. I was falling in and out of consciousness. On at least three separate occasions, I regained consciousness only to find myself kissing women or speaking to people I didn't even know, it made me feel incredibly edgy. So I fumbled my way through the hordes of people, looking for a good friend of mine named Julie; I finally located her dancing with some guy.

Pushing between them, I grabbed her by the arms saying, "Julie you've got to help me, I'm losing it big time!" Sensing my distress, she took me by the hand and pulled me to one side. Placing her hands on my face, she stared into my eyes, "Martin, what's wrong babe? Is everything ok?" Feeling uneasy, I told her, "Julie, I don't want to be here anymore, please, can you take me home?" Reassuring me, she said, "Of course I can, come on, let's get you out of here." She grabbed my hand and led me out of the apartment.

When we got outside, and onto the landing, I grabbed the rails and took deep breaths. I think the oxygen mixed with alcohol made it worse. I sat on the floor, and Julie stood over me, she stroked my hair while trying to calm me down. That's all I remember. The next day, I woke up in the living room of Brian's flat. I had a massive headache, and was well hung over.

When I got up, everyone was banging on about how I was the life of the party, and raved on about what I had done last night. Someone said to me, "I think you need to speak to John mate, man, he's a real mess." While attempting to get my bearings, I couldn't help but ask, "What's wrong with John? What do you mean he's a mess?"

Their reactions worried me. They just shook their heads as if to say; this has got nothing to do with us! Somehow, I managed to frighten the life out of John, and he wasn't speaking to me. The same person, who doesn't scare easily, had finally been broken. When I finally caught up with him back at my place, he told me the story:

"As the night went on, you were kissing all these girls and was having a blast. All of a sudden you got into a state about being the DJ at the party. I didn't understand what you were on about, so I took you outside to talk to you. You were in a real state about this DJ thing, but as I tried to calm you down, without warning, you suddenly grabbed me and lifted me up on to the balcony railing. I screamed at you to stop, but you then pushed me off the edge and dangled me over the balcony by my legs, shouting, I want to DJ! I want to DJ; I thought you were going to drop me."

I didn't know what to say; I was in shock! The balconies in those flats are about 80ft high, with a solid concrete pavement below. I couldn't remember any of this, but it had shaken John up pretty bad. I couldn't apologise enough, and was genuinely sorry · I know I could have killed him, and wouldn't have known.

"His nose was missing"

Later that day, I had a good hard think about what happened, and it was then I believe I had what some would call... a moment of clarity. Standing in my bedroom and looking into my mirror, I suddenly had an unexpected conversation with myself. Looking into my own eyes, I said, "You have to stop this Martin, you are going to kill yourself." It was at that very point I had an awakening. I turned away from binge drinking, and never looked back.

John was still drinking himself into extinction, which created a separation between us. He went out at night while I stayed home, and he'd come back smashed in the early hours of the morning. He always made a complete racket, and that started to get on my nerves. I knew at some point I'd have to address it, and have a word with him. So one evening I waited up and had my speech prepared; it got very late, and while waiting I fell asleep.

Suddenly my mobile rang, which startled me and woke me up. I answered, and it was the hospital; they had John there, and he was severely hurt. I gave them my address, and they dropped him off outside. When he came in, it was evident he had a broken nose. I wasted no time in asking, "John, What happened to your face?" His story was typically mental. On the night of the party, it reminded him of an old girlfriend who lived in that area, so he thought it would be a good idea to pay her a visit. Because it was late, he didn't want to knock on her door, so he decided to climb onto her balcony and knock on her bedroom window instead. Now to him, that made perfect sense, but considering it was several years since he'd last seen her, it didn't make any sense at all. Her husband didn't take it lightly, finding a strange man standing on his balcony, outside his bedroom window. So he decided to punch John, and broke his nose.

I sat down with him and tried to explain, "John, you can't just assume stuff, you need to get your head in order mate." He seemed to listen, but I wasn't sure how much of it was going in. The next evening he was off out again, and this time I gave him a strict warning, "John, behave yourself, do you hear me... I'm not kidding now, I mean it!" To which he replied earnestly, "I promise I won't do anything stupid, I'm just going out for a quick drink; I won't even be home late." I wanted to trust him, but just couldn't.

He didn't come home that night, and I knew that could be good or bad depending. It was in the wee hours of the morning, when I heard him come in, and something was wrong! John always came into my room to see if I was awake, especially after a night out, but not tonight. So, quickly jumping out of bed, I opened my door to check on him. He was quietly creeping up the stairs.

I couldn't believe the sight: the whole front of his face was smashed! His nose was missing, and it looked like his face had caved in. I carefully took him downstairs and sat him down. There were bruises all over his head and face, and he was having trouble breathing. It was a mess.

I immediately called an ambulance, and he was rushed in for emergency surgery. I sat on my sofa with my head in my hands staring into space, trying to get my head around all of this. I was there until daybreak. The next evening, we were all in our local pub, hanging out with friends, and I was stood at the bar ordering a soft drink. I leant on the counter, and had a little look around as you do while waiting. The entrance door swung open, and I got the biggest shock of my life! It was John; he came through the doors as casual as you like, wearing a hospital gown underneath his favourite mac.

He coolly stood next to me at the bar, and ordered himself a bottle of Stella. I was still in shock! I stared at him as he faced forward, waiting patiently for his beer. He had tape on the sides of his face, holding two clear tubes that were coming out of his nostrils. They had blood trickling through them and he looked a sight. He finally got his beer in hand and without a care in the world, turned to me holding his bottle saying, "Cheers Martin." I didn't know what to do; I was still coming to terms with the sight in front of me.

"Time to get my head together"

So I answered, "Cheers John," and he suddenly started to giggle; He looked like a mentally deranged person, escaped from a psych ward. I couldn't hold it any longer and cracked up laughing. We were both in stitches as blood bubbles popped out the tubes in his nose. It was disgusting and hilarious at the same time. People in the pub thought we were nuts! Well, only the ones who didn't know us. Our lot would've seen that as standard; we laughed so hard I nearly broke a rib. When I finally managed to sit him down, he proceeded to tell me what happened...

"I went back to the same flat where I got my nose broke the last time, definitely drunk and not thinking straight. I wanted to see my old girl again, and pulled the same reckless stunt as last time, climbing the balcony to her flat. But this time, her husband met me armed with a giant padlock. I tried to explain, but he wasn't having any of it. He laid into my head, nearly knocking me unconscious. As my arms came down, he smashed the metal lock into my face, obliterating my already broken nose."

"Flipping heck John," I said worriedly, "Why'd you have to go and do that again, didn't you learn your lesson the first time?" He just sat there shaking his head with a smirk on his face. That's what worried me about John; I never knew how much information he took in, he always smiled and got on with it. We finished off our drinks and took a slow stroll back to my place.

As we walked, I knew we couldn't go on like this, and decided it was time for us to have a heart to heart. Once inside, I gave him a chance to settle in, and made some tea. To be honest, I think he knew what was coming; it was in the air. I told him it would be in everyone's best interest, if he found somewhere else to live. We weren't good for each other, and although our friendship was strong, it somehow brought the worst out of him, or the bad out of me. I never studied chemistry in school, but knew enough to concede that ours was dangerous.

For someone who got kicked out of places all his life, he took it well; for him, it was an easy transition. I gave him a few days to sort himself out, but he disappeared without a trace the very next day. Things were quiet for a while without him, and to be honest, I needed time to get my head together. With all the craziness we went through, I missed him a lot, and still considered him a good and very loyal friend. But this wouldn't be the last time I'd see him.

"I'm going to bury you there!"

Several weeks later, some of the guys at the pub were telling me about a nightclub they were going to, and they were eager for me to come along. "You'll love this place, Martin, it'll be right up your street." I had ended my resolution to stop binge drinking and was now hitting the gear (steroids) pretty hard. Mixing that with alcohol and the occasional spot of acid.

I was just coming off my first ever bodybuilding competition, The Mr. & Miss Capital City. I was riding that high, and celebrating regularly. Clubs weren't really my thing, as the pub was fulfilling all my needs; girl's, alcohol, and good music, all the boxes were ticked. But always up for a new adventure, I agreed, and with my mates in tow, we left the pub and headed to this nightclub.

We got inside, and the atmosphere was electric! Although it seemed a lot smaller than I expected. To the left, there was a bar with two pool tables, and a decent seating area. The bar ran from there, and straight into the main area of the club. The dance floor was in the middle, with the DJ booth to the right with seating either side.

At the back of the club, there was a cocktail bar which was closed down; I soon found out this was a space for people to have a puff or do some class A drugs. My friends were excited I came to the club and were very keen to show me a great time. The atmosphere was pretty relaxed, and I enjoyed myself a lot. But as usual with the people I knew, there would always be trouble. One of our friends rushed over to us shouting, "There's a problem outside, and you all need to come out!" So we stormed out of the club, and straight across the main road to a housing estate; faced with about eight or nine Irish travellers. Quietly counting heads, I realised we were relatively even in number, which was a consolation.

As the dispute continued, it became apparent, there had been an altercation several weeks earlier involving my friends and these travellers, and this was the prearranged second leg. Contemplating the situation, I thought to myself, this is why they invited me, isn't it? Busy with my internal dialogue, I somehow got caught up in the centre of the argument; one of the travellers noticed I worked out, so he whipped off his top and got right up in my face.

"I could stay and fight"

The exchange was limited, as I couldn't understand a single word he was saying, plus it had nothing to do with me. But the bit I did catch was his finger pointing at the ground saying, "Ya see you? I'm going to bury you there!" I just smiled, keeping my eyes fixed on him in case he made a sudden move. Closing the distance (I learnt that people couldn't hit as hard when you're closer to them), I responded firmly, "Is that right mate, let's see it then?" Just as we were about to go at each other, a loud screeching sound filled the air; it was the police! And they came from everywhere.

We split up in different directions, as the police randomly selected their targets. Trying to look as casual as possible, I walked away as the police pounced on people around me, but I somehow managed to slip through the net. I quickly headed into the nearby poorly lit housing estate, and was relieved I hadn't been caught; I didn't fancy spending the night in a lonely cold police cell.

As I navigated my way through the property, I suddenly realised I was on my own in an unacquainted estate. There was no telling what could happen to a person in a place like this. So, I decided to return to the club and see if any of my friends were around. Trying to get my bearings, I turned a corner and standing right in front of me, were all the travellers we had been arguing with... and they saw me!

With only seconds to think, I had a difficult decision to make. It was hard trying to concentrate at that point, as my life was now flashing before my eyes. I had to weigh it up swiftly; if I run, they'll come after me, and that was no use, as I was unaccustomed to the estate. I could stay and fight, but that was a little unrealistic considering the numbers, or I could negotiate. Ever tried to negotiate with a traveller? No one could win that! Then it dawned on me.

Do the most unlikely thing possible to throw them off. So, taking a deep breath, I marched assertively towards them; looking a little-confused one of them shouted, "So... you wanna fight do ya?" With my poker face on, I thought, oh come on leave it out. I don't know if it was nerves or just a natural reaction, but I just started to laugh. The travellers looked startled, paused, then, in a synchronised roar, all broke out in laughter too.

We ended up talking and sniggering about the whole situation. I'm telling you, I have never been so relieved in my life. Managing to pull myself away from my new traveller pals, I found one of my friends near the club. He quickly told me what happened, "Martin, the police have arrested most of our lot, let's get down the station and wait for them to be released." And I agreed.

"Levels of exposure to violence"

There was something about these nights that excited me. I went back to the same club a couple of times after that, and couldn't help noticing the doormen were not that great. One of them took a bit of a dislike to me, and we got into a face-to-face confrontation, and that led into a short staring contest.

Standing my ground, and turning to one of his colleagues, I asked, "Where's your manager?" They must have thought I wanted to complain. So, answering reluctantly, one of them said, "One minute," and called the manager over to see me.

When he arrived, he said politely, "Yes sir, can I help you?" I quickly got to it. "Yes you sure can, do you think I can get a job here?" Looking puzzled he responded, "Excuse me?" So I repeated the question, "I'm asking you if I can get a job here?" Sensing my cockiness, he answered more firmly, "Well mate, what makes you think you could work here?" Pointing back at that bouncer, I said, "Because if he can do it, then I can!" I meant every word of it. Plus I could use the money too. The manager had an intrigued look on his face and paused taking some time to think...."Get here early next Friday, and we'll take it from there." He said decisively. Result! I was ecstatic! Looking over at the other doormen, I shouted, "Yes!" while rubbing my hands together as I walked away. The job wasn't even mine yet, but I was sure my show of confidence wouldn't hurt my chances. I knew that job was in my hands.

The following Friday, I turned up nice and early full of enthusiasm. As I walked in the club, I waited at the bar and as the manager approached, he could see the look on my face, I just couldn't stop smiling; I was fully wound up and ready to go. He played it cool and didn't give much away, asking me, "Do you wanna drink?" I nearly said, "I'll have a beer and a shot please," then realised why I was there. "Yeah sure, I'll have a pineapple juice please." He shouted over to a barmaid, and she brought us over our drinks.

"It was a free-for-all"

He spoke to me about the position, some of the situations that could arise, and how I would deal with them, etc. I explained to him that I knew how to look after myself, and told him I could handle it. I was then given a start the following week. He must have been playing hard to get, because no sooner had I swigged down that fruit juice, the job was mine. Talk about easy money. All relationships and interruptions were out of the way, so I had nothing to lose. That allowed me to put my whole life into working at this club. It was about to become my new life, and I went about it meticulously.

I already had years of pent-up aggression inside me, due to the levels of exposure to violence I had as a youngster. My patience had zeroed out by now too, as I became more and more intolerant of people or things that irritated me. I figured it would manifest itself sooner or later, especially with the amount of abuse you took on the door. I did snap a few times, punching people for refusing to drink up or launching punters out the door for not leaving the club quick enough. Some of the other doormen were starting to get annoyed with me, which frustrated me even more. I thought we were meant to be a team, but that wasn't the case.

I did have my fair share of good nights at the club, but they were mostly chaotic; the real enjoyment was being at our local pub. It had a great sense of family, and everyone stuck together there, but at the club, it was a free-for-all. The incidents here were not always predictable, and could go off at any given time.

"Aren't you going to do something?"

On one occasion, some of the doormen called me to assist them with a customer. I went out to see what was going on, and it was a guy and his girlfriend; he had taken the white pool ball from the bar and was holding it. One of the doormen said, "He left the club with the white ball and is refusing to give it back." Evaluating the situation I said, "Why have you called me for this when there are four of you out here?" There was no answer.

By now I was already pretty upset, thinking this could have been sorted out between them. I hadn't realised that two of my friends followed me out to see what was going on. Wanting to bring this petty drama to an immediate end, I stood there holding out my hand and asked politely, "Come on mate, give me the ball." But he responded angrily, "No, you come and get it!"

So I grabbed his hand and tried to get the ball from him. He had a firm grip and wouldn't let go. I twisted his arm, which bent him over, as I tried levering his fingers open. It was at that point one of my friends got fed up with it all, and kicked the guy full blast in the face, sending him crashing to the ground.

It was this kind of situation that frustrated me; none of this had to happen if everyone did their job. But no, it was all on me again. Yes, I retrieved the ball but was now incensed too. So in a temper, I threw the ball at him as he lay there, hitting him in the head and bouncing across the road. Then that old familiar sound... Silence. Somehow my actions were distasteful to everyone.

I couldn't care less and stepped back into the club with my pals. This club needed organising, the attitude of the doormen was a joke, and something had to change. I arranged a meeting with the manager, and gave him an outline of the issues that needed addressing.

118

Some of the bouncers chatting up girls, some who think they're Bruce Lee, and others at the first sign of trouble disappear to check the toilets. And finally... four bouncers struggling to deal with one unruly customer. What is that all about? I'd seen it all. The manager was a little shocked, but shouldn't have been surprised.

As we were coming to the end of the 80's, the landscape of the club scene was changing rapidly, with the emergence of house, trance garage, acid house, etc., meant the atmosphere in the clubs went with it. Different crowds bring different situations, which need capable people. And we just didn't have the right bodies for this job. It wasn't long before he allowed me to bring in my own crew, and I did, reliable guys that I could trust.

The club picked up and was getting busier each week. We had large crowds of people coming through the doors, and the club seemed to turn a corner. Of course, we had our usual issues with drunks and the odd fight here and there, but we were making a good living.

On one particular Saturday evening, there was tension in the air; you could just feel it. A rough group of guys showed up at the club, and I had seen them before, and taken a mental note. Because I didn't like the look of one of them, and I'm sure he didn't like the look of me either. So, I decided to take the lead, and have three others nearby in secondary position.

I gave him a customary pat down, but as I knelt to check his trouser leg, he kneed me in the chest, knocking me to the ground. As it happened, two of the other doormen stepped in, but I told them it was okay. I looked at this guy who stared blankly back at me and waved him into the club.

They were confused. "Aren't you going to do something?" They asked inquisitively. "Nah, it's all good," I said confidently. He thought I'd let it go, but no. I was giving him enough rope to hang himself... and wanted to see what he had come to do.
That particular evening the club was buzzing! Which meant positioning men strategically, especially on a full capacity night like this. I was covering all bases and made a stop at the most tedious section of the club, the poolroom. Commonly used by college students playing pool and falling asleep on the small round tables.

There wasn't much for me to do, so while keeping an eye on the tables, I took the time to have a natter with one of the barmaids. It was hard to hear anything she was saying, as the music blasted out of the dance area.

"Someone punted me in the side of the head"

I detected the sound of raised voices coming from inside the club, which was entirely reasonable for an evening of this magnitude; the ravers would frequently cheer, blow whistles or even shout as they partied hard. I glanced over at the bouncers stood at the entrance, to see if there was any reaction, but all appeared ok. Just to be sure, I ended my conversation, quickly finished my drink and got ready to take a look. But no sooner did I place my glass down; I heard a loud shrieking noise.

A barmaid came rushing from inside the club screaming "Fight! There's a fight; please help." I saw two bouncers leave their posts, and rushing into the club; it was going off now for sure. Heading in there from the well-lit bar made it difficult for me to focus, the club area was dark, and the combination of dry ice and strobe lights made it even harder to see. I crashed through the throngs of people shouting, "Coming through, coming through!" It took me a while to get my bearings.

The screaming sound in the distance became my guide, and I used it to navigate me through the crowd, as my eyes tried to focus. Finally breaking through the crowd, I found myself in an open space; my attention was immediately drawn to a guy holding a girl up against the wall, while others stood to watch; her face was covered in blood, and she looked dazed. Relieved someone was trying to help her, I slowed down; but quickly got a shock.

The guy holding her up placed one hand on her throat and drew back his other hand. He clenched his fist and punched her full blast, smashing her head off the wall and sending her lifeless body crashing to the floor. My feet couldn't carry me quick enough as I charged straight at him; he was brazen enough to come back at me too. Once we got a hold of each other, I instantly recognised his face; it was the guy from earlier, the one that kneed me in the chest; I couldn't have been happier.

I had no intention of getting him in the usual headlock; at this point, I was going to beat him into unconsciousness, and I think he knew it. I never realised the others standing by were his entourage, and they all rushed me, surrounding me in a pile of bodies.

Fearing the possibility of getting stabbed, I forced myself to the ground taking them with me; I was trying to create a little space. I gained some ground and although I was being punched, I still managed to get on all fours. But just as I was about to get to my feet, one of them kicked me full blast in the side of my head. It blasted my ear, and I blacked out.

"Making wild threats to kill"

As I came to, I could hear screaming and shouting; some voices were calmer than others, I also felt restricted. Everything was spinning, and I felt disorientated. As I finally came to, I was on my feet with the DJ riding on my back. He was yelling, "Martin it's me, stop! Martin, it's me!" I then noticed other random people in the club rushing towards me; they had their arms outstretched frantically trying to calm me down.

What happened to me? Where is everyone? It was bizarre. The club was nearly empty, only a handful of people remained and some were injured. An ambulance showed up but not the police, as we couldn't call them; the clubs reputation was already in tatters as it was. The paramedics checked the poor girl hit by that guy, and they looked me over too. Because of the trauma I received to my head, they suggested a trip to the hospital for further checks, but I wasn't interested.

I took a seat at the bar, got a stiff drink, and listened to the DJ and some others replay the night's adventure to me. When I blacked out, I apparently went berserk! Running around the club screaming blue murder, while trying to grab the guy who hit that girl. They said I was like a heat seeker hunting this guy down with evil intent.

The doormen rounded up his friends and removed them from the building, but I wasn't having any of it, and just wouldn't let it go. The other doormen had to let him out, because I made wild threats to kill him and his family. They told me I completely lost control and no one could stop me; in my temper, I even shoved a female friend over a table, while chasing him. I felt terrible! And for the first time, I came to terms with the fact I may be losing control. Desperately seeking a change, it came in the form of an English-born Jamaican girl named Angie. I had seen her a few times; she usually turned up at the club towards the end of the night, but we were never formally introduced. Our introduction came while I was locking up one evening as people were leaving the building.

"Telling me about this Jesus"

She approached me and asked, "Sorry to bother you, do you think you could come with me to collect my younger brother from the police station, they will only release him to a responsible adult, and I'm only 17." I had never considered myself accountable, but as I was 20 at the time, that did qualify me as an adult. Not wanting to disappoint, I said, "Ok, give me a minute to lock up, and I'll go with you." If her face was anything to go by, she seemed chuffed.

Angie was a very chatty person, and that suited me fine. It took the pressure off me, and didn't leave room for awkward silences. The station was about a mile and a half away, and my calculations made it a 30-minute journey. I wasn't a great conversationist, as I always had stuff on my mind, which caused me to think a lot. As we strolled at 1am the streets were tranquil and dimly lit.

I found it relaxing, listening to her speak about her issues at home, and the trouble her brother caused. The street lamps were hypnotic; as they lit us up momentarily, every time we passed them. Finally at the station, I had no problems getting her brother released; the police were glad to see the back of him. As the three of us strolled back to their parents, I couldn't understand why her brother was so much trouble, yes, he was a cheeky little so and so, but I liked him; he was funny. Seeing as it was another 30-minute journey, we stopped off to grab a bite on the way.

I intrigued her little brother as he sneakily pulled faces at his sister; I pretended not to notice. When we arrived, Angie asked me to come in and have a hot drink, but I figured it was quite late and didn't want to disturb her parents. But she insisted, and wouldn't take no for an answer.

122

As we got through the front door, her brother hastily tried to duck into his bedroom, but his mum was already out of hers. Knowing the trouble her brother was in, Angie tried to head her off by getting in her way saying: "Hi mum, this is Martin." Ignoring Angie's weak attempt to deflect her, and in her broad Jamaican accent, she said, "Where is the criminal?" Meaning her delinquent son who was now trying to get out of her reach. Well, he didn't get far enough, and she walloped him all the way to his room.

"Stories from the Bible"

After she'd taken care of him, she casually tottered over to me and said politely, "Hello Martin," I whispered, "Hello, listen, I'm sorry about the time." She turned and responded while strolling back to her room, "That's ok darling." I found that amusing. Angie and I spoke for a little while, and her company was good. I hadn't done anything like this in a long time, and I missed it. As it was well into the am, I politely said good night and walked home.

Several weeks had passed, and we were both getting on really well. Angie started meeting me earlier in the pub, and eventually joined our entourage as we made our way to the club. Finally feeling comfortable, I invited her round to mums to hang out; Angie said she had a wedding to go to that particular night, but promised to come round before she went.

When she arrived, I barely recognised her; she was all dolled up and looked stunning. We sat up in my room chatting for ages, and we laughed a lot. I hadn't smiled in such a long time, and was finally beginning to let my hair down. It was time for her to leave, but I didn't want her to go · I was enjoying myself for once and didn't want it to end. The truth is, she didn't want to leave either, and ended up spending the night. Our relationship developed from there. I was working as a hod carrier during the day, on a site that was around the corner from my house.

Angie regularly came to see me with her friends, usually bearing a bottle of cold milk. She knew I liked that. As far as relationships went, I felt like I was ready to get more involved and started to let Angie in emotionally. I was still very wary about all that. Angie thought that now we were an item, it would be a good idea to meet her family. I was nervous and wondered whether they'd even like me. When I met her parents, her dad was very polite, although a little quiet, but her mum, my goodness she was an angel.

She grabbed me by the arm and led me straight into the kitchen, sitting me down at the table and offered me food; I love Caribbean cooking, so I was in heaven. While sitting there eating, her mum chatted away to me, and it wasn't long before I realised she was one of those born-again Christians. My old friend Paul was one of those too, and he did the same thing, always telling me about this Jesus.

When Paul told me stories from the Bible, it did bring me a little comfort, and being honest, I never really knew why it did. But listening to Angie's mum was different; she obviously had a lot of knowledge just like Paul; however, there was a significant difference between them. I picked up on that straight away... She spoke about him like she knew him personally. It was extraordinary to hear, but her conviction intrigued me.

"Imagine if this Jesus person exists?"

Angie went to the local shops to buy junk food, and had just walked in. When she realised her mum was speaking with me about Jesus, she went into one, "Oh Mum! Leave him alone!" But before I could say a word in defence, her mum quickly returned fire, "Angie, shut up!" But Angie wasn't about to let it go, and continued shouting back, "Mum, Martin doesn't want to hear it, no one does, just leave it alone." I didn't know what to do; I was stuck in the middle of two passionate Jamaican women, fighting over me for different reasons and very different agendas.

At that point her mum turned to me and said calmly, "You see Martin, you see the devil, you see how he works?" To which Angie replied, "That's right mum, I'm the devil... Oh, shut up!" Storming into her bedroom and slamming the door shut.

I took that as an opportunity to leave, thanked her mum for the food, and quickly said goodbye to Angie, who was still fuming. While heading home, the bible stories swirled around in my head and got me thinking; could all that be true? Imagine if this Jesus person existed? But with most things that clogged my mind, I shelved it and moved on. Working at the club became a dangerous occupation. For the first time, I took the odd evening off to empty my mind; the fights inside the club were becoming more frequent, and insanely fierce. I was losing it mentally, and needed to gain some clarity about where my life was going.

"I realised my lip was bleeding"

As part of that process, I thought it might be a good idea to attend the club as a visitor. Working on the door didn't allow you to enjoy anything. So once inside I told my manager, "Listen, let's not talk shop tonight, I'm here as a civilian." He just laughed and said jokingly, "Bloody heck Martin, what's got into you? Is that even possible?" I just smiled and shook my head. As we continued our convo, he kept glancing over my shoulder, and in a concerned voice said, "Martin, do you know that bloke?" I turned my head to have a quick look and replied, "Nah, never seen him before."

Right at that moment and without warning, the guy walked up behind me. My manager alerted me, and I quickly turned around to face him, "Do you think you are hard?" He said in a thick Irish accent. My mind went right back to my first night here, crap! It's those bloody travellers again! Assuming he may be a little inebriated, I said, "I think you've had too much to drink mate."

But as I turned to face my manager, he hit me in the mouth with his bottle of beer, and then bolted into the club. I quickly checked my face; and pulling my hand away, I realised my lip was bleeding. I saw red! Hurrying to the entrance of the club, I took a quick peek and noticed there were loads of them sitting at tables. I doubled back into the bar and grabbed the fully loaded 15kg Calor gas canister that was propping the door open.

After humping it up onto my chest, I sprinted towards the club as my manager and the other doormen waved their arms, frantically to stop me. Once I got in range, I let it fly into the club where they were all sitting. People nearby desperately tried to get out of the firing line, as tables and chairs flew into the air; the situation had erupted. I managed to grab myself a table, and worked my way into the club, as bottles, chairs and glasses rained down on me. I managed to make it to the cocktail bar at the far side of the building, in the hope that some of my younger pals might help out. Finally making it to the cocktail bar, I couldn't believe what I saw... nothing! There was no one. With no way out, apart from back through the angry crowd of travellers, I was now stranded. Still bemused at how empty it was, I moved in to take a closer look, and there they were; my so-called friends were hiding in the corners, desperately trying to keep out of the way.

"I was a wreck psychologically"

Becoming a little desperate, I shouted, "Guys, you gonna help me or what? There are loads of these bloody travellers." After everything I had done to hook these guys up, this is how they repaid me. "Leave it out Martin, this has nothing to do with us, what's wrong with you man!"

So there I was, faced with at least ten or twelve travellers, loaded with glasses, broken table legs and whatever else they could get hold of. For the first time in my life, I acknowledged this might be my last stand. Preparing for my demise, I felt someone grab hold of my trouser buckle at the back of my jeans. I glanced around, and didn't see anyone, but I could still feel it tugging.

So I looked again, only this time as I peered down, a young girl who was with one of the youngsters was knelt down behind me, holding onto my jeans. A little confused I asked her, "You ok?" Looking up at me, she said, "I'm scared!" Then put her head back down, while holding on for dear life. Now, I was in an awkward position. You see, I could easily take responsibility for myself, but I was now being made liable for someone else; that changed everything.

Overcome by a strong sense of fatherly protectiveness, I went into defence mode. Calculating the situation, I reached for a bottle and glass sitting on a nearby table. I broke them both and whispered to her, "Don't worry, we are going to get through this." Sincerely hoping we would. I kept my ground as the travellers approached, and they stood right in front of me, with the guy who hit me out in front. Without thinking, the words instinctively left my mouth, "Listen, you might get me in a rush, but I tell you this, one of you will be coming with me. So who is it going to be?" I meant every word of it.

126

The guy in front looked back at the others and mumbled something; I couldn't quite hear from where I was standing. There was an eerie silence, then without warning, the guy in front stepped forward and spat in my face. I was furious! Gripping the broken glass tightly, I almost instinctively stuck it in him, but suddenly remembered I wasn't alone. I kept telling myself, "Let it go Martin, its only spit, let it go." After another short silence, he looked me up and down, and dropped his glass to the floor. That prompted all the others to drop theirs, and they slowly started to leave.

"I had no sense of reality"

Right at that moment, the young girl behind me quickly stood up and wrapped her arms around me. She held me so tight; I was still holding the broken bottle and glass, so I couldn't return the embrace. She was so relieved, yelling, "Thank you, thank you so much." To be honest, I didn't know why she was thanking me; she probably saved my life. The thing is; if they had jumped me, I wouldn't have hesitated killing one of them. So maybe I should be thanking her.

Things at the club were starting to reach boiling point, and every weekend got worse. I was a wreck psychologically, and it was starting to affect me. My colleagues became a little worried when I started carrying a large hunting knife, and a medium sized hammer inside my jacket. I never intended using them, but had to be sure I could protect myself in this crazy and unpredictable environment. My only release was being at the gym, and that intensified.

It was the only thing that kept me sane. Well, at least that's what I thought. Drinking wasn't a serious problem, but I was stacking a cocktail of steroid injections, mixed with the occasional ecstasy tab and some acid. I had no sense of reality. For me, this was all life had to offer, and it was hard trying to keep myself medicated; it required serious funds to maintain this self-destructive habit.

An old pal was now running the club, and he gave me as much work as I needed. I was there every day and night; even on the nights no one fancied. Thursday night was Biker Night; a local biker gang congregated at the club, and lined their Harley's and custom choppers outside in the street. I loved those bikes.

These guys were clearly 'full patch' members. They wore faded Levis and leather waistcoats, with their chapter clearly displayed on the back. They were here to drink and party hard. This was my favourite night. I got on with every biker that came in, and they loved me. I never paid for a drink, as they always treated me to free alcohol. Thankfully, I never had an ounce of trouble on those nights, but it did gain me quite a reputation.

"It was all one big mask"

The morning was my time to get in early. I had to open up and prepare the bar; local workmen were about to rush the building, looking for beer and topless women. In the afternoon I was DJ for the strippers, and it was always the strangest time for me. It had nothing to do with naked women sitting behind the DJ booth with me, no. I had seen enough of that in my short lifetime.

It was the deep-rooted disappointment I had in them. You could see them preparing themselves to become numb and cold, enabling them to get through their demeaning routine. That made me sick! It was pitiful to watch; trying to look elegant and erotic as drunken, obnoxious, and often rowdy workers, abused them while getting their rocks off.

The most shameful part was watching them go round with an empty jar; practically having to beg for the money they'd just earned. I'd always sit and have a drink with the girls afterwards, watching them spilling out the jar, desperately counting the pennies. The sad thing was, these women were well educated, and had their whole lives ahead of them.

I asked that question to one of them, "Why are you wasting your time in this club, surely there are better ways to make money than flashing your boobs for a bit of cash?" Her response stunned me. "Darling, you've got to do what you've got to do." That comment was another brick in the wall of my increasing disillusionment with the whole female race.

I had never given up in the hope of finding love, but for me, it had to be real! But up to now it was elusive as ever. I had no time to whine, I had to mop up the spilt beer, pick up the broken glass, wash out the empty pint glasses and wipe down all the tables from the earlier shenanigans. The only peace I had was Sunday afternoon.

I would go to Angie's mums, and like clockwork, she fed me and gave me an earful of Jesus. I started to take some of it in, and it did bring some relief. I was well established with the family at this point, but my relationship with Angie was diminishing rapidly. Angie and I were no good for each other, and I lost count the number of punch-ups and cruel slanging matches we had. They were brutal! My emotions hung in the balance, and I was becoming a nervous wreck. I cried when I was alone, and at times became gripped with a sense of desperation and hopelessness.

"This volatile and unhealthy relationship"

I felt if I didn't keep moving, I would come to my end. So I took more gear, trained as hard as I could, and got involved with as many things as possible, from different sexual relationships to stringent debt collecting. But it was all one big mask. No matter how much I ran, I couldn't escape, and would have to face myself sooner or later. My relationship with Angie collapsed; my intense vulnerability and her trust issues made it impossible for both of us.

I urgently needed some relational stability, but looked for it in all the wrong places. I got myself into relationships I didn't even want or enjoy. At one point, I was seeing three different women at the same time, and one of them was Angie's neighbour Janet. We got talking one day, and it just escalated from there.

She had the kind of stability I wanted and needed, she had a place, and a couple of kids from a failed long-term relationship, but was very level headed and mature. We quickly formed a relationship, and as short as it was, Janet's presence improved my emotional state. That was until Angie walked in on us one evening, while together at mums. The door was unlocked, and Angie had a habit of walking in unannounced. Taking one look at Janet, she said firmly, "See ya," while pointing to the front door. Janet looked at me, and my face affirmed it would be best to comply. No sooner did Janet walk out and closed the door behind her, Angie flew into a rage.

"What is she doing around here? How did this happen?" Trying to explain it was pointless, when she was in a state. Before I knew it, she was backing me up, getting right up in my face. We reached the kitchen, and that was enough, I told her straight, "Angie listen, I haven't seen you in ages and assumed we had finished," and that's when she let fly. Angie didn't do scratching or pulling hair; in a rage, she threw punches with commanding force.

"Pulling a gun from his pocket"

Defending myself, I grabbed her closely to avoid her blows, and then my temper left me. Smashing into the cupboards and doors, we wrestled each other and ended up in the bathroom. During the ruckus, she fell into the bathtub and was trapped; she started screaming like a defenceless child. Now she was the victim! I thought it was pathetic! Standing on the spot looking at her, I'd had enough of this volatile and unhealthy relationship, and told her to get up and out of my life.

Several weeks later, I met another girl in the pub; she was Irish and moved into the area after splitting with her ex. Her name was Colleen, and she was gorgeous! After plucking up the courage to speak to her, we ended up back at my place, and spent the night together. We got on so well, and I was hoping she could be the one.

Angie wasn't around, but I did bump into Janet occasionally, as Colleen lived right around the corner from her. My dream was slowly coming back; sincerely thinking marriage and kids could be on the cards with Colleen. She was beautiful, calm and very kind, but she did like a drink.

It escaped me at first, but I soon noticed her spending a lot of time at the pub with her friends. It may sound like double standards coming from me, but I couldn't stand women who drank; especially after seeing what it did to mum. We fell out over her drinking, and my trust issues were starting to kick in again. It was brought to my attention that Janet's fella didn't take kindly to me being anywhere near her; he sent a clear message, "Come anywhere near my missus, and I'll cut your face up." Hearing threats like that weren't new to me, so putting it on the back burner; I plodded on with my own business.

However, the threats didn't go away and became more frequent. Living with paranoia and anxiety, there were only two ways for me to deal with this, wait or initiate. And I was never good at waiting.

I walked into his estate and right past his house, hoping we could get this sorted once and for all. He was washing his car outside Janet's, and spotted me, but said nothing, finding that strange, I popped into a local shop and bought myself a drink, but walking back, it all kicked off. He stood casually next to his car, and waited for me to get in range. Then pulling a gun from his jacket pocket, he aimed it straight at me. The sight of it startled me, and triggered my reflexes. Launching at him, I grabbed his arms as we wrestled back and forth, banging into his car and eventually hitting the ground.

"My body was now trembling uncontrollably"

As we landed, he ended up on top of me, and that was not a good place to be. I desperately needed an advantage. I reached under his thigh and managed to tip him over, allowing me to get on top. That's when I let fly. Without thinking or any restraint, I punched him repeatedly in his head, as he wriggled on the floor trying to avoid getting hit. Thankfully for him, his parka got pulled over his head and cushioned most of the blows, as he bellowed, "Get off me, get off me." I eventually came to my senses and let him go.

Grabbing him by his jacket and lifting him up I said, "Keep my name out of your f***ing mouth, or the next time you see me, it'll be your last." Right at that point, I noticed Janet coming around the corner with the kids, so letting him go, I walked away and quickly disappeared. Walking into the main road, I bumped into Colleen coming out of the pub. After chatting for a few minutes, Colleen grabbed my hands; she loved to stroke and hold them.

"Martin, what have you done?" She shrieked at the top of her voice. It made me jump. Looking down at my right hand, I noticed two of my knuckles were missing above my ring, and little finger; it looked like I had a golf ball in the back of my hand. The adrenaline was keeping me from feeling the pain, but it looked a mess. I wanted to go home, but Colleen wasn't having any of it; she was adamant we had to get to a hospital.

On the way to my place, we spotted a paramedic. He had just finished a home visit, so sticking my head into his car, I thrust my hand in his face, and asked, "Oi mate, is this serious?" Rolling his eyes and sighing, he took a look at it, and said, "Listen, if I were you mate, I'd get straight down to A & E." Colleen jumped in too, "Yeah that's what I told him." Feeling a little peed off, I roared, "Oh get lost the both of ya's," and stormed off.

"My head was killing me"

Colleen came after me and nagged me all the way home, "Martin, you need to get that seen to at the hospital, it looks severe." Feeling pressured and stressed, I suddenly stopped and grabbed her by the arms, "Listen, f****ing drop it alright! Just leave me alone." I then turned away and stormed off; Colleen stood on the spot watching me wander into the distance, not knowing what to do. I got back to my place and slumped onto my sofa. I lay there for about ten minutes, and there was a knock at the door. I got up to answer, and it was Colleen; she just stared up at me with tears in her eyes. "You'd better come in," I said, leaving the door open and walking back inside.

She didn't utter a word and lay on the sofa with me. The adrenaline wore off, and the pain suddenly got a lot sharper. But that wasn't bothering me as much as the shuddering in my body, which got worse by the minute; my body was now trembling uncontrollably. My breaths were getting shorter, and sweat poured from my brow. It was time to get to the hospital, so we called a cab and left. On arrival, they took one look at my hand and rushed me straight into a room, and sent a specialist in to see me.

They gave me something for the shock, and then a long-winded talk about what the procedure would be. A nurse entered the room and took out a syringe with a long needle on it. She injected me between each finger, and around the lump. Needles never bothered me; my friends and I injected each other all the time, so that was fine. They took me for an x-ray and finally brought me back to the room. But now there were four nurses present. Pulling out the radiograph and holding it up, she showed me the damage. "Ok, so you've broken both your little finger and your ring finger, you've also shattered the entire right side of your hand."

I listened carefully as one of them said in a calm voice, "Martin when I touch this can you feel any pain?" She softly squeezed my hand and the pain was slightly dulled but still hurt. So not wanting to be misunderstood, I said firmly, "Yes, I can still feel the pain."

Grabbing a near by gas cylinder, she put the mask over my face saying, "Here take deep breaths while we look at your hand for you." Doing as she advised, taking big gulps of gas, she prodded at my hand, and man it was painful. Then strategically placing each nurse around my body, she went for it!

"My stress levels turned into panic attacks"

Grabbing the back of my hand at the base of my wrist, she clamped down and pulled hard and slow. The pain was unbearable! I had never screamed as loud as I did that night; Colleen even heard it from the waiting area and rushed into the room. By the time they finished, my head was killing me and I couldn't focus on anything. They took me for another x-ray, and the specialist told me, "Mr Berry, we've done our best to save your hand and knuckles.

However, one of your fingers will have to be reset." Unwilling to go through any more of that pain, I refused, "No way, I'm not going through that again, it can stay as it is." Looking a little concerned, he then said, well, you could end up having problems with"... I interrupted sternly, not allowing him to finish. I wasn't interested. "That's fine mate, it can stay as it is!" He just shook his head, closed his notes and let me go. Colleen and I were on and off, as my stress levels got steadily worse, and developed into panic attacks. Poor Colleen couldn't keep up with me, and it was heart-breaking not being able to spend more time with her.

The shame of my erratic behaviour made me clam up; I just didn't know how to be vulnerable and share my issues. So, keeping my distance and isolating myself was the easiest solution.

CHAPTER 7

MIDNIGHT TRAIN TO NOWHERE

There was a big rave coming up in the New Year, and because of the sheer magnitude, many security firms had to be involved. A rave of this size meant it had to be at a local sports centre, so we had the task of assembling our teams.

As we were one of the firms asked, I gave it some thoughtful consideration. Picking the right team for a job of this size cannot be rushed. Taking on a job like this you need to know who you're working with, just in case anything goes down. So taking the lead, I needed a few faithful men to come on board. The first two were going to be easy; I had a couple of reliable and dependable guys from our club, which left space for one more.

"Someone's been stabbed"

Then it came to me, I know someone who would love to be involved. He's a bit of a loose canon, but if my back was against the wall, I know he could be trusted... John! It was a chance to show him how much I cared by giving him this opportunity, and as expected, he jumped at it. The truth is we all knew it could all go wrong, but if we had to go into battle, I wanted John with me.

The evening was mental; they called a briefing with the owners and at least two hundred bouncers - it was going to be the biggest New Year party in history. We were assigned our posts, and got ready for the opening. I put two guys on the exits, and John on the main floor, while I gave oversight, walking around the building, keeping an eye on everything else.

People flooded the building, and the large open space quickly filled up. The rave was incredible! You could barely hear yourself think over the loud sound system, as coloured laser lights streamed across the walls and dance floor. People bopped while jumping up and down, with drinks and glow sticks in their hands. While taking it all in, my attention was drawn to a doorman from another firm. He was having a word with a couple of guys; observing their body language, I tried to make out what was going on. From what I could see, it looked like they were smoking a joint openly, and he'd gone over to have a quick word. It rapidly got heated, and an argument broke out between them; that's when I moved in.

The doorman didn't take kindly to their rude behaviour and grabbed one of them by the arm. His other friend tried to interfere, and I jumped in. But no sooner had I intervened, I took a punch in the face, so I backed up. This guy continued trying to hit me, so I moved out the way, while trying to assess the situation. You don't want to go steaming into a fight like that, especially when you can't tell how many people are involved, or whether they have weapons or not.

So realising there was only two, I went about restraining this guy by holding his arm behind his back, as the other doorman got into it with his friend. While holding him, he started giving me loads of lip, then without warning, the bouncer turned his attention toward us, and head-butted him in the face as I held him; nearly knocking him unconscious. It was all getting out of hand. So I picked him up and took him to the medics by the exit, that's when I noticed the police. They were everywhere.

Rushing back into the club, the place was in chaos! Police pushed through the crowds as people screamed while running in different directions. I got two of my men together, but couldn't locate John. Then one of them told me, "Martin, someone's been stabbed, we don't know if it was one person or many, that's why the police are here." My first thought was John, so I asked, "Have you guys seen John at all?" They just looked at each other and shrugged their shoulders. I was hoping he wasn't involved.

The rave was eventually shut down. We were all gathered to get our pay, and that's when I found him. There were many arrests and some of the doormen were arrested too. I grabbed John by the arm and pulled him to one side, "John, this is one of those times you need to be very clear about what you say, do you understand me?" He looked a little shocked and wondered what was going on, "What arc you talking about Mart, what's going on?" That's when I got serious. "John, don't mess me around, where were you? We all know you weren't here!" And thankfully he opened up, "Yeah sorry, I didn't want to say anything to you, because I knew you would get mad at me. My missus lives around the corner, so I occasionally ducked out to see her."

Believe it or not, I was relieved that's all he'd done. I started to laugh, "So you didn't do something you shouldn't have to anyone?" He just smirked and said, "What? Are you crazy, Nah, I'd just gone to visit my bird." I was so pleased I could have kissed him. And because he told the truth and was honest, I paid him in full. We finished up the night at another New Year party and celebrated in style. I didn't see much of John after that, and left him to get on with his life.

Two months had rolled by, and my 22nd birthday was coming up. People were hassling me for weeks about having a party at my place; after all, we already used their homes to accommodate us rowdy thrill seeking lot, so it was my turn. Mum was in Italy, and that provided the perfect opportunity.

"There was a bang at the front door"

So with the date set and a friend agreeing to DJ, all we needed was some bodies on the door. The only problem was, trying to gauge how many people were going to show up, that was a difficult one; we advertised it and left it at that. The party was in full swing as I finished up at work, so after grabbing a few friends, we arrived at my party.

I couldn't believe the sight! Not only was it in my house, but also in both my front and back gardens, and spilling out about three houses down. Going inside, and seeing the hordes' of people, I couldn't believe we managed to cram that many into such a confined space; it was incredible.

The place was heaving, and the music was loud! While doing the rounds and mingling with people, a girl I got talking to suddenly started feeling dizzy and unwell. I got her some water and took her outside for some fresh air.

136

Once outside, she began to feel worse, so I led her to the kerb and she began to vomit. I was rubbing her back, and right at that moment Angie showed up. Just my luck! Someone had told her I was outside, and when she spotted me with this girl, she saw red!

Without warning, she pulled me around, broke the chain off my neck and nearly took my eye out with her fingernail. We quickly got into a fistfight outside in the street, and wrestled each other as people tried to separate us. As always she played the poor little victim, and I didn't bother trying to explain. I went to clear my head and calm down.

On my return, the house was a mess. There was some redecorating needed for sure, or mum was going to kill me. People slowly trickled out of the party as it wound down, and a few friends stayed over to sleep the day through. Including the girl who was sick. The day was breaking, and the birds were singing, when suddenly there was a bang at the front door.

"Why did you have to push it?"

We all ignored it thinking it was some latecomers. Then we could hear shouting, "Oi! Open the door; I know my bird is in there. Open up!" By the time I got to my feet, two of my pals were already on theirs. Quickly putting two and two together, there was only one equation; it had to be the sick girl. "Is that your boyfriend?" I asked firmly, she just sat quiet and sheepishly nodded her head.

That didn't help me, so I changed tack. "Do you want to leave?" She finally broke her silence, "I do, but I'm scared, I don't know if I want to be with him." It was turning into a real life soap opera, which wasn't my style. So navigating my way through the maze of empty cans and rubbish, I got to the door and opened it.

As I did, her bloke was standing there brandishing an axe. That's when it came to me; it may not be a good idea for her to go with him right now after all. He tried to push past me, but I blocked him as he shouted, "Where is she? I know she's in there!" Trying to peek inside. Pushing him back and pulling the door closed behind me, I reassured him, "Listen mate, she's not here, I know who you're talking about, but she left about two hours ago."

You could see he wasn't buying any of it, but I had to get rid of him for her sake. He got louder and more agitated, which was drawing the attention of my neighbours. That got me aggravated, as I listened to this angry and madly insecure guy.

Trying to resolve the situation, I stepped towards him. As I did, he lowered the axe gripping the handle saying, "Touch me, and I'll axe you!" That surprised me. "What? I sniggered. He then repeated himself, "You heard me... touch me, and I'll axe you!" I looked around, and one of my friends was edging his way out the front door, I shook my head ever so slightly, and he stopped, but stood there just in case.

Looking back at the angry young man, I asked inquisitively, "Are you sure you're going to axe me?" He was confident, "Yeah positive." If he were going to hit me, it would have happened already, so sensing he wasn't in his right mind; I asked him one more time. "So, let me get this straight, if I touch you, you're going to hit me with that axe?" He answered decisively, "Yeah that's right." One of my pals was chuckling behind me; he knew what was coming next.

I planted my feet, but he was too busy making threats to notice. Before he could move, I clocked him straight in the face sending him to the pavement, as his axe bounced across the concrete. He scuttled around the floor reaching for his weapon, as I stood over him yelling, "Why didn't you just leave when you had the chance mate, why did you have to push it?" He eventually got to his feet with his axe and staggered around making more threats. "Man you've had it, you just wait, you'll see," then ran off into the distance.

We waited a while to make sure he was gone, then told his ex-girlfriend it would be a good idea for her to leave too. Knowing this could bring trouble to mums door, I decided to find the pub where this guy hung out, and get this beef sorted once and for all. After finding it, I headed inside. To my surprise, he was sitting there with his girlfriend; they had apparently made up.

When he saw me coming towards him, he had a look of shock and surprise on his face, quickly jumping off his stool. But before he could say a word I interjected, "Listen, I'm sorry about what happened, but what do you expect when you bring an axe to my door and threaten me with it. He looked even more surprised, and then I noticed the left side of his face was swollen. I switched into big brother mode. "Man, look at your face! Why did you make me do that? It didn't have to happen that way you know; you could have left it alone."

He just sighed and said, "Yeah I know, I just love her so much, I didn't know what to do." Putting my arm on his shoulder, I gave him a tip; "Yeah you do, just don't turn up at a house brandishing an axe, that'll help!" He broke out in laughter, and said, "Come on, let me buy you a beer." We sat drinking for quite a while, and it was helpful to know that this particular drama was over.

"My bell was well and truly rung"

I hadn't told anyone about my feelings of disillusionment, anger or the anxiety I felt which was bottled up pretty well. I wasn't enjoying anything, and always felt frustrated at what the world had to offer. A good friend of mine named Steve was running the club at that time, so we pretty much did whatever we wanted.

We hung around after closing time with different girls. We drank crazy amounts of alcohol, played music on the decks, and got up to no good. I was in a downward spiral, and my old dream of being married; having kids, and the white picket fence was well and truly gone. Sex and drugs mixed with copious amounts of alcohol became my only form of expression. I used every sexual experience to give me the attention I needed, then moved on.

I'm sure my attitude was affecting those around me too, including mum and Susan. We were always having problems at home, and the arguments were non-stop. Until one day it got completely out of control. Some people wanted me dead and were intent on getting it done. It wasn't long before there were a couple of failed attempts on my life.

The first one was close, but the second was too tight to mention. You see, this lifestyle brought all kinds of unwanted attention; so I went into hiding and officially ended my unhealthy relationship with the club. At the end of my rope, I brought Angie round to stay with me, but mum was having none of it. She hurled abuse at me, "You are not wanted here, so why don't you take your stuff and get out!" That continuous and often repeated statement wore me out. Angie was embarrassed, but I told her to ignore it. We went upstairs and into my room.

Susan, being the instigator decided to come up and push my door open. "Go on, why don't you just get out, you're not wanted here!" Sitting on my sofa bed without looking at her, I said calmly, "Get out of my room and leave me alone." She didn't listen and just carried on hurling abuse. My stress levels were already through the roof, and I was trying to stay calm, but finally lost my temper. I jumped up and grabbed her, pushing her out the door, but as we reached the hallway, mum was outside waiting with a broom handle, and started hitting me with it.

I completely lost control and blanked out. Susan screamed at me to let go of mum, as I had her in a chokehold and was slowly squeezing the life out of her; she was slowly passing out. When I realised what was happening, I quickly let her go, and she slumped to the floor. I knew things were getting out of control, but this was stupid. I had to get out of this house, but had nowhere else to go.

The next day, mum continued her barrage of abuse, but I was still not listening. Mum had a way of getting her point across though, and it came in the form of a great big marble ashtray. She began kicking off about how much she didn't want me in the house, and that her family didn't like me either.

Mum even told me my uncles were coming to beat me up. At one point, she even brought my brother into the mix, and told me how much he hated me too. We eventually got into a massive slanging match, and I had enough. I decided to leave and headed for the front door. But halfway through the doorway, BASH! I felt this almighty thud on the back of my head, nearly knocking me unconscious.

I staggered forward, as my eyes were blurred; my bell was well and truly rung. Looking up, I saw half of the marble ashtray land on a car parked outside. I grabbed my head, which was killing me, and I could feel it swelling in my hand. As I took my hand away, blood dripped from my fingers; it was pouring out of my head like a tap. Frozen with shock; I stood there feeling woozy from the loss of blood. As I watched mum screaming at me, all I could hear were muffled noises. I felt angry and a little queasy, so glancing down and seeing the other half of the ashtray, I quickly picked it up. Without thinking, I launched it into the living room window.

I then grabbed the other half, and threw that piece into another side of the window. It wasn't a good idea, because Susan was in there with her newborn, and it could have hit either one of them. To be honest, at that point I didn't care. But thank goodness it didn't.

"I felt physically sick"

Intent on never going back, I moved into a squat with my old friend Peter. He was now homeless too, and it was a great opportunity for us to have a place we could both call home. It was unfurnished with no electric and only gas. We slept in the front room and left a gas ring burning to keep us warm at night. During the day, we went to the supermarket to buy sausage meat squares for £1 and some bread.

After spending the day wandering the streets, we'd come home to make sausage meat sandwiches. It didn't taste brilliant, but man it satisfied the hunger. We eventually ran out of money and ended up broke, so we had to beg for money to get food. That was degrading for me, as I had always worked for my money. My mate Paul gave me a big protein powder tub; he saved his coins in that and told me to use it to sort myself out. His brother Darren gave me some money too, which was a massive help.

I went straight back to Peter who was now asleep. I woke him up and treated him to a kebab in the high road, although I was careful to keep some money back for supplies. Several weeks went by and things were getting tight; hungry and dirty, I was desperate to be back home, even though they didn't want me.

I just missed sleeping in a bed and cleaning myself in the mornings. Peter and I were asleep; when around 5 am in the morning, there was a mighty bang! It was the police; they kicked in the door and came with a warrant for Peter's arrest. They handcuffed him, bundled him into a van, and threw me out on the street. Peter was sent to prison for four months, and I now had nowhere to live.

I didn't know what to do, and knew mum wouldn't have me back, but I had to do something. So after walking around aimlessly until evening, I was hungry and tired. I had to do something, so I tried my luck at Billy's, and knocked on his door. He came to the window and noticed it was me.

Opening up he asked, "What are you doing around here at this time of night?" I explained to him what happened, but he just said, "Look, go round to mums, she might let you back in, you never know unless you ask." I assured him, "Billy trust me, that's never going to happen, I just need a place for tonight. I promise, I'll only stay one evening." But he wouldn't relent, "Leave it out Martin, I don't need this right now," and shut the door.

After standing there for a few minutes, I didn't know what to do. There were only two choices: Go round to mums at this time of night and make her mad, or stay where I am. My mind was made up; I'd have to sleep on the steps outside Billy's place. The staircase leading up to his door was covered, so at least it would shelter me from rain, but it offered nothing in the way of heat.

It was freezing cold. I lay on the smooth concrete floor near the night-light on the stairwell. The icy cold floor, and spiders running around kept me up for most of the night. It was now morning, and I felt physically sick. I was starving, and couldn't shake off the intense cold feeling in my body.

"I had lost my will to live"

Lying still on that hard concrete for most of the night stopped my circulation and left me feeling sore and weak. Knowing mum wouldn't have me back, I had no choice but to walk around my old neighbourhood. I looked for friends or anyone who'd give me some money, and I managed to get someone to give me £1 for a can of drink and a mars bar. They tasted like heaven.

With nowhere to go, I rubbed my cold fingers together, and tried to figure out what to do next. I felt sick, and the chill was getting worse. At this point, even if I had somewhere to go, my body was far too weak to get me there; I needed to sit down somewhere warm. Out of desperation and with zero energy, I took my chances and went to mums. Knocking on the door, I stood there nervously waiting for a verbal onslaught. The door opened, "What do you want?" She asked. Staring right at her, I answered humbly, "I'm hungry mum, can I please come in and eat something?" (Now mum could do a lot of things, but she couldn't see people go hungry). She invited me in and told me straight, "You can get something to eat, then I want you out!" I wasn't about to argue, "Ok mum, that's fine." She then quickly ushered me into the kitchen.

I was fed and watered, and as I still had clothes there, was even allowed to get myself cleaned up. I got a little comfortable, and tried talking mum into letting me stay, but she was having none of it. In the end, she gave me some money and told me that I had to give it back soon. It was very generous, but I didn't know how I would ever get the money to pay her back. I would just have to cross that bridge when I came to it.

Some time had passed, and I moved around a lot staying with different people. Even Angie would sneak me into her parents' home occasionally while they were asleep, to help me out. I eventually went back to see mum, and we managed to get along while having tea together. She asked me about the money she gave me, and I told her I didn't have it. She wasn't happy, and that exploded into a full-scale argument.

I did have some money on me, but I was going to need it considering my situation. So, feeling angry and humiliated, I took the money out of my pocket and threw it in her face. "Go on then, take it back you tight b***h!" Mum was making tea for herself, and was now holding a kettle full of scalding hot water. In a blind fury she tried to throw it over me, and I had no choice but to react.

I grabbed her arms and pushed her to one side, trying to avoid the hot water. She dropped the kettle while falling forward, and put her arms out to break her fall. She missed the chair she was reaching for, and hit her face on the way down. I couldn't look. I wanted to defend myself, but never intended to hurt her.

It was a good idea to disappear, so I made myself scarce and went missing for a while. I eventually ended up at Billy's house, and wanted to talk to him about what happened. Mum had already beaten me to it, and told him I attacked her. He came to the door

and said, "What do you want? Come round for some more have ya?"
Mum was standing in the hallway behind him, and her face looked
terrible. I didn't know what to say. He then pushed past me saying,
"Come downstairs into the garages - I want to show you something."
I knew what was going to happen, but didn't care.

As I approached the garages, Billy pulled out a lump of wood. But
before he could say anything, I took off my jacket, removed the rings
on my fingers, and walked right up to him. Part of me wanted him
to smash my skull in; I was looking forward to it. Sensing I had lost
my will to live, he suddenly stopped. "Why are we fighting like this?
What's going on with you Martin?" I tried to explain to him what
had happened; after all, he knew what it was like in that house.
"Martin, do yourself a favour, get away from here, and get out of
that house. I suggest you go and never come back."

My mind was made up. Liverpool was to be my destination, but I
didn't know why. There was only one person to say goodbye to, and
that was my best mate Mark. We met up and spoke about all the
things I went through, and he was shocked. You see, I never
actually told Mark about what really went on in my life, as I figured
he'd be disappointed with me; I truly looked up to him.

"Where are you going?"

Angie found out about my trip, and didn't like the idea at all. She
threw a fit, so I let her drop me off at the train station so she could
say goodbye. We argued throughout the whole journey, and it
continued right up until I got on the train. That's when she finally
broke down in tears.

As the train pulled away from the station, there was a profound
sense of relief. I finally started to relax, and eventually fell into a
deep, well-needed sleep. On arrival at Liverpool Lime Street, I
hadn't thought about a place to stay, or anything else. I was just
glad to be away from all the chaos that surrounded me, not to
mention the noise going on in my head.

I moved around from place to place, and managed to stay with some
family. I still never managed to settle, but that wasn't anyone's
fault, it was just my state of mind. All I needed was time to unpack

my thoughts, and a little room to move about. I didn't feel I could do that with family around me. But as long as there was no chaos, and no arguing, I knew I'd eventually be okay.

One afternoon while hanging outside my cousins, a neighbour of theirs asked if I would like to babysit with her. I didn't even know who she was; her name was Katy, and she wanted me to come over to sit her younger sisters with her. So having nothing better to do, I agreed and went over. It had to be the weirdest situation ever. I was sitting in a family's home, with people I don't know from a bar of soap; I felt like a plum. They were a big family; five girls and one boy, and from what I heard, her dad was a massive bloke, so I didn't want to cross him by overstaying my welcome.

I stayed for most of the evening. They bombarded me with questions about London and my funny accent; but although we were having fun, it was getting late, and I politely made my exit. Katy didn't want me to go, and asked me to stay until her parents came home. There was no way I was going to do that, and managed to slip away.

The next morning, I stuck to my usual routine of keeping out of people's way, walking to the local sports centre and taking a swim. That's where I spent most of my time, and then went back to my cousins'. Later that evening, I was asked to babysit with Katy, and again I agreed. This night was going to be different in lots of ways, good, bad and a lot of cringe factor.

We were sitting watching the TV, while the girls and their brother entertained themselves, Katy asked me if I would like a cup of tea, so I politely said yes. Then, while handing it to me, the cup managed to work its way free from her hand, and landed right in my lap. I jumped up with a cry, and she was genuinely apologetic.

She suggested I take my trousers off, so she could put them in the tumble dryer, but I was having none of it. I could just imagine their mother and father walking in while I was standing there in my boxers - no chance! I opted for the old hair dryer job and dried my trousers that way. Eventually, the laughing and giggling stopped, and I began to relax again. Katy must have warned her parents about my early exits, because just as I was getting ready to leave, I heard someone coming through the front door.

My heart was in my mouth when she said, "Oh, that'll be Mum and Dad." I just froze! Her dad walked into the room, and I realised she wasn't telling lies - her dad was big and looked pretty mean too. Her mum was very quiet and smiled politely. "Alright mate," her father said in his broad scouse accent. "Yes thanks," I replied, quickly followed by, "Well, I'd better be on my way then." But as I was getting ready to leave, her dad said, "Where are you going? Stay and have a cup of tea," so I agreed and sat back down. The conversation was great, and I enjoyed talking to her dad, we seemed to get on very well.

It was now quite late; so trying to make my exit again, her father stopped me. "Wait, where are you staying?" I responded casually, "At my cousins." Quickly jumping back in he said, "Sleeping were?" I had to think, "Err, on the sofa; it's no problem at all." Without hesitation, he said firmly, "No, you're not, get your stuff together, you will stay here with us - we have the room."

"I wanted her to have the best chance"

I couldn't believe what I was hearing - they didn't even know me! It felt strangely ok. This was the place where no one knew me, and they gave me a fresh start. I got my stuff, and her dad made an extra room for me with his son and an older daughter, while the younger girls roomed together. I even went to the dole office and transferred my details to Liverpool, ready to settle down.

I continued my daily routine by keeping out of everyone's way, swimming and keeping myself busy. I was finally starting to feel at ease, and couldn't be happier. Every morning Katy got up early in the morning to clean the house, and I watched her do it. There was a serene quality about her, and she carried a tranquillity that was therapeutic; she relaxed me, and it was special. I told her that I could easily marry her, and that she would make someone a beautiful wife, and it was true. We got on very well, and I know my life was the better for it. But, with every up, there's always a down.

Angie and I were still in contact with each other, and she got upset with me being away. She broke down in tears in the hope she'd convince me to come back, and it worked. The constant barrage of complaints forced me into coming back to see her, and man, it was the biggest mistake I ever made! I travelled all the way from Liverpool, and went straight round to her place. But when I got there, she acted like there was no big deal. She even told me she was busy, and didn't really have time to see me.

I couldn't believe it! She was driving me nuts! I told her where to get off, and decided to get straight back to Liverpool. Angie offered to drop me to the station again, and as usual, we argued all the way there. Man, it was soul-destroying! It was now starting to ruin my time in Liverpool, and I knew it wouldn't be long before I'd end up having to make another move.

A good friend of mine contacted me saying there was a driving job going at a builder's yard, literally around the corner from mums, he had me intrigued. I didn't have any work in Liverpool; however, I was finally getting my head together thanks to this amazing family. Desperate for a bit of work, I decided to check it out. It was a timber company, and they were looking for a 7.5t driver with experience. Although my license had the entitlement, I had never driven a 7.5t truck before. So, with nothing to lose, I applied anyway, and they gave me the job.

That meant moving back to London. So I called Katy in Liverpool asking her to send my driving licence and other papers for the job, which she did. Things worked out with the company, and my friend allowed me to move into his for a while. I loved my time in Liverpool, and will never forget the hospitality of that unique family, and the way they treated me like a son.

Thanks to that wonderful family, I was now prepared for regular home life again. Katy was the one who initially reached out to me, so I didn't want to lose contact with her. I invited her to London, and was excited to see her again. Deep in my heart, I was sure we could've made a go of it.

I always dreamt of being married, and as far as I was concerned, she was absolutely perfect. But once Katy arrived, something changed, while out together, I just couldn't shake this peculiar feeling. You see Katy was the model of everything I'd ever wanted, but I knew that would all change once we were together. I was damaged goods, and I knew she deserved better.

It was one of the hardest decisions I would ever have to make. There was no way I'd be responsible for ruining her life. I wanted the best for her, but unfortunately, I knew that meant keeping her away from me.

I'll never forget that moment we met, and her incredible family that took me in. They gave me a fresh start in life, and so did she.

CHAPTER 8

THE END IS NEAR

The nightclub was eventually closed down, and taken over by the church next door. Mark met a young Irish girl and was smitten; they moved in together, and had a baby boy. Mark was understandably more tied up with family affairs now, and after finally making peace with mum, I alternated my stays between her and my sister Susan.

Susan had just met a guy named John. He had just been released from prison and was trying to go straight. He seemed friendly enough and was very easy-going, so it seemed like a good idea for them to get together. Especially after her previous failed relationship, which left her on her own with two kids. I figured it might help them both to settle down. So he moved to London, and they got a council house not far from me.

"Come on Sue, we're going home"

It wasn't long however, before I noticed there was a lot of money coming into the house, and that made me suspicious. John had no job, and was regularly out and about, which made me think he was grafting - in other words, stealing. I gave him a personal warning; "Don't let me find out you're giving my sister drugs! I won't be happy if you do." He swore to me that it wasn't the case, so I stayed out of their business.

The two of them went missing, leaving the children with mum. The social services intervened, and sent them to their biological father in Liverpool. Susan finally came home after John ended up back in prison, and we were all fed up with their destructive pastimes. Mum came up with a good idea; take Susan to Italy for the summer, to help her get her head together. It proved to be a good move, as Susan responded well to the mountain air, and looked healthier by the day.

But she was soon up to her old tricks again, returning to England to see some friends. She promised mum she'd be back soon. However, two weeks had passed, and there was no sign of her. I eventually returned home to check on mums, and got the shock of my life. The smell was incredible, but nothing compared to the unbelievable mess inside.

There were dirty cups and plates of food smothered in mold, randomly placed around the living room. Piles of used syringes, still filled with blood, were strewn all over the floor, with random clothes scattered over the furniture. It was a complete state. Sitting there surveying the room, with my head in my hands, I decided to get it sorted. Starting with the living room, I gathered up all the used syringes and bagged them, before cleaning the dishes and tidying the clothes. It was ages before the house looked habitable again. Now I had to find Susan.

I went on a mission to find her, starting with the streets of Kings Cross; including the train station. After pounding the streets and asking countless people, I came up with nothing. Needing something to drink, I headed back into the station to find a shop, and that's when I saw her. Deep in the far alcoves of the station, I could just about make out a small figure slumped on the floor.

She was semi-conscious, scruffy and very dirty. Until that point, I was furious, but now I was filled with sadness and deep disappointment. How could she prefer this crappy life, compared to living in the Piedmont Mountains of Italy? Kneeling down and shaking her a little, I said to her calmly, "Come on Sue, we're going home." I lifted her back to her feet while she mumbled to herself. No matter how many times I rescued her, she went back out on the streets and did the very same thing.

"It was like a reoccurring nightmare"

It felt like a never-ending battle. I was constantly rescuing her from the dealers who were trying to protect their source of income by keeping her hooked. I just couldn't keep up with it all, and was completely worn out. Then one evening, she made a reverse charge call to me from a phone box. She rarely did that unless she needed money or food, but not tonight. Some guy had beaten her severely, and brutally burned her face and body multiple times with a lit cigarette. I called a couple of friends, and we drove to Kings Cross to get her, with the intention of finding that bloke, and beating him within an inch of his life.

We searched a couple of streets and quickly located her; she was cowering against a glass window at the station. Rushing over to her, I noticed a few guys sitting on the railings to my right, and another couple standing near by. I wondered if one of them was the coward, while kneeling down to get a closer look at her. I lifted her face as she tried to cover the burns.

A surge of fury ran through me like a torrent; I wanted to go ballistic, but just closed my eyes and took a deep breath. While kneeling down, my attention was abruptly interrupted by a voice behind me, "Anyone of you boys got a light?" I couldn't believe the audacity. Then it came to me, "Wait! He just asked for a light, could this be the guy?"

I looked up at his reflection through the window, but before I could even focus... THUD! One of my friends punched him full-blast in the face, knocking him to the ground. They both punched and kicked him across the floor, as he tried to get back to his feet. His friends looked on in shock, not wanting to join him. I was very tempted to jump in, but decided to enjoy the show instead.

Things only got worse from that point, and Susan ended up in prison. I visited her regularly and she would cry, as she constantly felt depressed and lonely; it ripped me apart. The problem for me was, I didn't know what was better for her – being inside or out. She was always in some kind of trouble, and would ring me for money or food.

It was breaking my heart seeing her in such a horrible state, but there was nothing I could do. Susan was now critically ill, and was spending time in and out of hospital. Mentally fragile and trying to keep it together, I tried to create some distance between us. Holding down a full-time job, while dealing with this madness proved difficult; it was like a reoccurring nightmare. I wasn't sleeping well, and managed to find another job working nights at a local transport company. It was a very tough and physically demanding job, but having something to concentrate on made it easier to bear.

The evenings were getting pretty cold, and winter was well and truly upon us. Angie was still on the scene, turning up to my workplace from time to time. I never really understood why she did, as we weren't together anymore. Although she did give me the occasional lift home, which stopped due to her turning up half drunk and ranting on about our old relationship. I hadn't seen Angie for quite sometime, and was wondering what happened to her. While out one evening, I bumped into her, and she told me something that surprised me.

She had turned up at my workplace one night while I was in the canteen; and was beeping outside. A close work colleague named Henry went over to her and said, "Listen Angie, why don't you leave Martin alone, and let him get on with his life? I'm sure you've got better things to do with yours." When she told me, I couldn't believe it, what a good friend!

"That evening was surreal"

His family were in London for the weekend, and they invited me out for the night. They arranged to go to a bar restaurant which wasn't far from where I lived. We had an excellent time chatting about life, and shared some interesting stories. Realising they had bought all the drinks, I insisted they let me get a round in. So standing up and walking over to the bar, I stood up on the foot rail and glanced down at the barmaid. BOOM! It hit me.

While looking down at her, this short petite and beautiful young woman gazed back up at me. Something happened. I cannot explain it; it was like finding the missing piece of jigsaw in my life. I remember the exact thought I had that night. 'I like her.' I had never felt anything remotely close to this before. The direction of my life was about to change forever.

After seeing her that first time, I knew there was something different about the way I felt. I spent that next month continually going to the bar to see her, desperately hoping she'd notice me. I went so often; even the manager let me stay behind for afters. I found it difficult to speak to her, because whenever I got close, it made me feel all funny inside. I decided to pluck up the courage to ask her out... She said no! Man that hurt!

I found out from her manager that her name was Sandra, and she had also just come out of a bad relationship. Getting rejected like that would usually make me run a mile, but not this time. I was completely undeterred. I walked by her workplace every day on my way to the gym. So while going past, I saw her in the distance walking towards me. I knew if I could just get to talk to her, she'd see I am not that bad. So looking into a shop window, I waited a minute or so, before turning around.

She was gone. I took it hard, assuming she must have seen me from a distance and avoided me on purpose; that knocked my confidence. During that week I saw her again, but this time we spoke. We spent the afternoon sitting in a local park, and got to know each other better. I saw her a few more times, and she finally agreed to go out with me.

On our first date, we went to the West End and walked around the scenic parts of London. We had a great evening chatting about stuff, and then finished up at my place. Mum was in Italy at the time, so the house was empty. We stayed up talking for hours, and she agreed to stay over. As I walked into my room getting ready for bed, she looked at me funny. "Where are you going?" Not knowing how to respond, I just said, "Well, you know." She was having none of it! "You can sleep downstairs." I got my marching orders. That evening was surreal. I lay on the sofa thinking about this unusual situation, while she slept comfortably in my bed.

"Things got physical"

I woke up early and made breakfast for us both. We spent the day together, and she agreed to come out with me again the following night. After another pleasant evening, we got back to my place, and I was rewarded for my endeavours. She let me sleep on the sofa, again. The next morning I asked Sandra to move her stuff in, and she did.

We were in love, and now living together after only two dates. It worked out well for a while, but it wasn't long before we were in trouble. Spending all my time with Sandra made me dependent again, and that's when it all started going downhill. My past came back to haunt me, and again, that led me to distrust.

Because of my past hurts, the closer I got to Sandra, the more anxious I became and slowly started to unravel. I evaluated her love for me by putting her through a stringent set of tests, all born out of my own insecurity and anxiety. It put a considerable strain on Sandra. We agreed to go to Italy to get away from it all, but because of my destructive behaviour, she made a decision to go to America instead. Obviously I was devastated, but didn't know what to do about it. She had made up her mind, and I had to get used to it. The next few weeks were the worst. I accepted the fact she was going, but wondered if I'd ever see her again.

Finally, the day eventually came. Sandra had her bags packed and was ready for America. The thought of her leaving was too much for me, so I took her to the train station and let her go to the airport on her own. When I got home, I lay on my bed, holding the shirt she wore while staying with me. It still had her smell on it. Our time apart put a lot of emotional strain on me, but I knew I deserved it and sucked it up.

"She was in a horrible state"

While Sandra was away, I spent all of my time between work and the gym. I used loads of gear to keep my mind focused; I got physically stronger, but it didn't do my head any good. If I didn't have something to focus on, my mind would race and I got very tense and edgy. My anxiety was exacerbated at work, by the constant jibes about Sandra having an affair in America. Things got physical with my good friend Henry; he wouldn't stop joking about her, and we got into a physical fight. I just couldn't get those horrible thoughts out of my head, and was really missing her.

Several months had passed, and after hearing nothing back from Sandra, I began to think she wasn't coming back. My cousin invited me to Liverpool, to hang out and get away from it all. So I borrowed a car from a friend and drove up for the weekend. I took my good buddy Michael with me; he always had the ability to cheer me up.

The weekend was great, but there I was again, rambling on about Sandra. I even carried a photograph of her in the car. We arrived back in London around 8pm, and went straight out for something to eat. As we stood outside a shop on the high road, Angie appeared with a friend and two other guys. When she saw me she said cockily, "Come up to see your girlfriend have you?" I was intrigued by that comment. So I asked, "How do you know about Sandra?" She then said, "Oh, is that her name then?" It sounded as if she'd recently seen her. "Why are you asking? Have you seen her?" Angie paused momentarily, "Yeah, she's at her usual place."

Wasting no time, I grabbed Michael, and we rushed to the bar to see for ourselves, and there she was. My heart was in my mouth, so I approached with caution. "Hey Sandra, can I see you after work?" She didn't seem too excited to see me and said, "Ok, I'll see you after." Seeing her in the flesh again did something to me, and I just couldn't wait to be with her again.

Later that evening, we drove round to her mum's house and chatted outside. Something had changed; she was cold towards me, and it was like I never knew her. During the conversation, she said, "I'm popping indoors," and off she went. Thinking she'd be back soon, I waited for a while, but she never returned. It wasn't going as I'd planned, and it was too late to knock, so I left it. The following morning we met again, and it was pretty much the same thing. It appeared the more vulnerable I got; the more she enjoyed it.

That week I was rearranging my room at mums, and Sandra came to help me. Emotionally, I was clinging on with my fingertips, but just didn't want anyone to know. But it eventually came out while cleaning my room; mum had a gripe about something, and I lost my temper. "You know what? Why don't you both get f****d! Go on Sandra; you can go too!" I was just worn out, and couldn't take anymore.

Suddenly there was a shift. Sandra's attitude changed, and she became affectionate to me. The situation calmed down and we managed to finish the evening well. Sandra and I began to get along, and things were going great. Yes, we had our ups and downs, but that never stopped the way we felt about each other.

Several months later she got pregnant; we were going to be a family. I told her it would be best to tell her parents on her own, out of respect for them, and she agreed. An hour later, I received a call from her, and she was in a horrible state.

She was crying uncontrollably, and asked me to come as soon as possible. Getting to the house as quick as I could, the confrontation began. Sandra's parents were obviously very upset, and we all said things that were not very helpful. That started the steady breakdown of my relationship with her parents.

Sandra was now heavily pregnant, and was given temporary accommodation. Our first child was on the way and I was getting nervous. Sandra was in the maternity ward about to be induced, so I decided to spend the whole night by her side. She just wouldn't go into labour, and thought it best for me to go home. She assured me they would give me a call when it was time to come back.

No sooner did I get home, I received a call for me to return. But with the lack of sleep, I passed out on the bed. Finally waking up, and realising some time had passed; I jumped on my trusty Claude Butler mountain bike, and rushed to the hospital as fast as I could. Arriving at the entrance, I jumped off the bike and let it smash into the nearby railings.

"The cracks started to appear"

Reaching the ward and entering the room, I saw our baby boy lying on the weighing machine. The nurse brought him straight over to me, and I was the first to hold him. It was an incredible feeling holding my firstborn; it felt awesome. I sat next to Sandra and watched in relief as she rested; she had been through so much leading up to this, and I was proud of her. We named our first son Aaron.

Sandra and I muddled our way through, and things were ok for as long as they could be. We had our fair share of arguments, and were no different than most couples our age. She was only twenty at the time, and I was twenty-five. Neither of us had any experience to fall back on; we were learning on the job. Not long after Aaron was born, we were expecting baby number two, and I wasn't in a good place mentally or emotionally.

Regular family interference was another contributor to our problems, and that just intensified things. Every time we had an issue, Sandra's dad would intervene; he'd come round and just sit there without saying a word to me. I found him rude and always felt judged; he never got to know me on a personal level, and I felt like he didn't want to either. To be perfectly honest, I only put up with it for Sandra's sake, because if I had my way, it would never have gone down as smoothly. Nine months had elapsed, and our second son was born; we named him Dean.

He was born at home – and it was an exciting and scary experience! It was over so fast, that by early afternoon, baby Dean was sleeping. Aaron stood over his cot, wondering how he appeared, as Sandra got some well-earned rest. Now that baby number two was finally here, and that focus was out the way, I was looking for my next fix.

Preparing for the upcoming Mr Titan bodybuilding competition would do it, so I put all my energy into that. It was my first time competing clean; I hadn't used any gear, and was completely natural. On the night, both Mark and Peter won their classes, and I came a measly third, although I did win best presentation. I decided to retire from these competitions, as I was just not willing to juice myself to death for a plastic trophy; there had to be more to life than that.

"I'd broken down"

Now with two children, we were given a bigger place to live. It was a lovely one-bedroom flat, which wasn't far from our previous apartment. When we moved in, it felt like home; we had a separate bedroom and a large living room, with an adjoining kitchen. It gave the boys enough space to roll around in their strollers.

The excitement of our new place concealed a lot of pressure that was building; no sooner had the sheen wore off, the cracks started to appear. Sandra was suffering from depression and the doctors didn't offer counselling, but tried filling her with Prozac. That annoyed the life out of me, as they just weren't helping her.

My issues were reaching boiling point, and something had to give. Mum was back and forth to Italy, so I disappeared with her for weeks on end, leaving Sandra with the kids to pick up the pieces; I did that a lot. I don't know why I couldn't speak about my feelings;

it was probably because of embarrassment or shame. I just couldn't open up, but it finally came out when I got to Italy.

Mum and Lino were arguing about him smoking in the car, and they got into a massive row over it. I couldn't take anymore, and screamed at them to stop! They both looked at me in shock, as tears streamed down my face; I cried uncontrollably for hours. I'd broken down.

The thought of arguing or fighting drove me insane, and my head felt like it was going to explode. The stress of everyday life was just too much for me.

CHAPTER 9

A WRETCH LIKE ME

We eventually moved into a two-bedroom council house, and carried all our problems with us. Our children were growing fast, and we needed a little extra money to live a decent and comfortable life. I got a job at a local catering company, and as always, there had to be some kind of drama going on. The company were hiring drivers right in the middle of a strike. That meant I had to pass through a picket line every morning, which they built on the industrial estate.

We also had security with us constantly, just in case we were attacked during work. It was a crazy job in many ways. I started at 4.30am and sometimes didn't finish till 9 or 10pm. There was no sick pay, no overtime and no paid annual leave. I borrowed money to buy a car; not only did I need a vehicle to get to work, but also a place to sleep. Sleeping in the car was my only guarantee of being first in line, which got me back at a reasonable hour. It wasn't much of a life, but at the end of the day, it did give Sandra a little bit of financial freedom, which meant she didn't have to worry.

"Something was not quite right"

I slowly made enough to pay all the bills, which allowed Sandra to keep her own money and the benefits for the kids. My boss was taking damages off me for the truck, which would sometimes leave me skint. The Saturday morning run gave me an opportunity to earn £30, to put in my pocket, which I regularly did. After an intense five-day week, the extra morning took its toll.

The job ruined our weekends, and always prevented me from doing anything with the family. I always felt drained and unable to move, which left me feeling demoralised. There was a big walk-in freezer at work, and it was the size of a small warehouse. We were never provided with protective gear, and if we wanted to get loaded on time, we were expected to go into it.

While out delivering in Essex, I felt a pain in my back, which was niggling me; I thought it might be the driver's seat. But by the time we got to the next delivery, it was hurting so bad I could hardly stand. My body was now starting to convulse, and my driver's mate was getting worried. I headed to the next delivery, but wasn't able to make it; the pain reached a level I had never experienced before.

Clinging to the steering wheel in severe pain, I said, "Paul, please direct me to a hospital sharpish!" He had to give me instructions, as I couldn't even see the road properly, so he told me when to turn and when to go straight. We eventually made it to a hospital, and Paul jumped out of the truck and ran to get a medic. The pain had me so rigid I could hardly move. The doctors managed to get me out of the truck and into a wheelchair; then rushed me straight into the ward.

Paul called work, and asked them to come and pick up the truck. While Dr Jelly finger checked me inside and out, he said he couldn't find anything wrong with me, and loaded me up with painkillers. Although I could still feel the pain in my upper back, he just seemed confused and put it down to strain. The advice was, go home and rest.

I was finally home and the pain subsided. The family had already eaten, so I headed round to the Chinese. Not long after finishing my food, nausea hit me like a truck, and I vomited violently. Slumping to the living room floor, Sandra rushed over to check on me. "Hey babe, is everything ok?" (Sometimes I lay on the floor because it helped my back). I still wasn't sure, so I just nodded my head.

After resting there for a while, I realised something was wrong. "Sandra! Get an ambulance!" She looked down at me, "Are you sure?" I felt the urgency, and I just knew it wasn't good. "Yes, please do it now!" She called the ambulance straight away, and they arrived within minutes. Once in the house, and on closer inspection, they realised what was wrong.

Before I knew it, they had put two drips in me and rushed me off to A&E. I was taken straight in and prepped for surgery. My body was convulsing violently, and I was coughing up a greeny-brown substance. They decided not to operate, and relied on the drip they had given me; they put me on 24hr observation. It turned out to be bronchial pneumonia. It had caused a blood clot on my lung, and the medics said it would have killed me, if I had remained on my floor for another two hours. The drip they had given me was to water my blood down and hopefully break the clot up naturally.

My stay in hospital was surreal. On arrival at the ward, I was placed next to an old Jamaican gentleman who was crying out at the top of his voice. "Please Jesus, don't take me, please Jesus, I'm sorry for everything I've done, please Jesus don't take me now." He called out for ages. Seeing him so desperate broke my heart. Jesus had come up so many times in my life, so I said under my breath, "Please help him Jesus, he really needs it. And if its not too much bother, I could do with some help too."

Well, I must have caught a blessing that night, because my recovery was nothing short of a miracle. I hadn't taken any of the medication they gave me, but stored it up in my bedside table. My improvement was off the chart, and went up like a rocket. Within one week I was out of the hospital, although anaemic and half my normal weight. A week had passed, and my boss called asking me to hurry back to work. Taking his instruction, I went back, but it was way too early. I couldn't lift a thing and had the energy of a gnat, so that was me finished. After two years hard labour, enough was enough; I quit.

"It's over, it's all gone"

While doing deliveries, I made friends with a man who had his own catering business, and he asked me to join him. It was a small company, and he wanted me to do sales to build up the business. Working in that area for two years meant my knowledge was excellent, and I had become good friends with many of the shop and business owners. He promised me a significant amount of money by way of payment, and I wasn't about to let this opportunity pass me by. So we shook on it and got straight to work.

After months of hard work and negotiations, we increased our client load, expanding the business. Having more capital meant we could rent the building next door, so we knocked the wall through and made it into one big warehouse. We invested in a brand new Mercedes Sprinter van, and were now receiving most of our stock in bulk from major suppliers. We surpassed all our expectations, and the company was booming. Within the first year, other companies were looking to merge with us, and negotiations were on going. With all the travelling to and from potential customers, I needed a company car, so we got one on hire purchase. That freed up another van for the increase in deliveries.

Things couldn't have been better. Sandra and I were already planning what we'd do with the extra money, and scheduled some things we could do with the kids. I took a minimum salary, while thinking of the long-term benefits; I figured they would be generous. But it had come to our attention; one of the office staff had been secretly collecting outstanding customer debts. The final figure was around £10,000; they took the money and quickly left the country.

We managed to pick ourselves up, and I was assured it wouldn't affect the business. To alleviate any fears, he even hired extra office staff. Months had passed, and things were ticking along perfectly or at least that's what I thought... My boss had been frequently attending meetings at the bank, and I figured he was just organising the finances, as that was not my strength.

We had just finished dinner, and Sandra was upstairs putting the kids to bed. My phone rang; it was my boss and he didn't sound happy. "Can you come straight into the office tomorrow morning Martin? I need to see you." I didn't sleep well that night, and a million things went through my head. That morning I took Sandra with me, and we headed straight to the office.

Walking inside, he was sat at his desk looking utterly dejected; he had two of our drivers seated in the room with him. The suspense was killing me, "What's wrong?" I said, desperately trying to figure out what was going on. What he said next nearly knocked me over.

"It's over, it's all gone," he said wearily staring at the table in front of him. "Wait! What's gone?" I asked probingly. "Everything! - We are bankrupt!" Stumbling for words, I was trying to understand what went wrong. "But we had so much money coming in, and were doing fine, the vehicles, the customers. I don't understand." He just sat there silent. Slowly realising where this was going, my blood started to boil.

"If the business is truly gone, then I want all the money you owe me now!" He stared at me with a blank look on his face, quietly repeating himself. "Martin, there is no money, did you hear what I said... we're bankrupt!" Looking over at Sandra, and seeing the look on her face, made me want to kill him. It was all gone! There would be no money, no holiday or anything good for Sandra or the kids.

I wanted to die. Knowing it was futile trying to argue or fight, I just gave in. Taking the keys of the company car out of my pocket, I slammed them down in front of him, and said firmly, "You sort this mess out." Lucky for Sandra and I, one of the drivers was just leaving and offered us a lift home; we lived a long way from here, and I wasn't really expecting to come home without a car. It later came to light he was sending the money back to his own country. He had purchased all the stock on credit, deliberately bankrupting the business.

"He resembled a Viking"

The effects of losing that money were immense; we had prepared for so many things, and it all went up in a puff of smoke. Sandra was very supportive and understanding, recognising I just wanted to get it right for us. Without any solid education to speak of, employment opportunities were limited, which meant I had to take whatever I could get. Struggling to find work put pressure on me, as I always worried about the family finances, and wanted to make sure that Sandra and the kids were ok.

That always caused arguments between us, and created a lot of tension in the home. I even considered starting my own delivery company, but had my fingers burned so bad I just couldn't go there. All the failed attempts at doing good left me feeling unhappy and dissatisfied, and it put a considerable strain on our relationship; we were at breaking point.

The poor children didn't understand what was going on. They watched us fight and argue all the time, but finally, there was a breakthrough. I received an offer from a firm delivering sandwiches throughout the night, and it was perfect for me. I hadn't slept properly for months, as the feelings of anxiety and nervousness were back again.

This job required working on your own initiative, and I thrived on that. I had a company van with a fuel card, keys to the warehouse, and a regular route. Another bonus was when the kids were on holiday; I could take them out on deliveries with me. They were always given free sweets by the shop owners, and thoroughly enjoyed the adventure of driving at night.

Financially more secure, I decided to fulfil a lifetime dream... Take my full motorcycle test. After finding a company to learn with, they arranged a finance deal so I could pay in instalments, and then booked my test date. They booked me out for three full days, with my test on the forth. My instructor was really experienced, and helped me pass first time; it was such a great feeling.

Now that I had my licence, it was time to get some wheels. After scouring the bike stores, I eventually spotted one; a silver Yamaha XJR1300 and it was big! I bought it on finance and was super excited. Sandra loved the bike as much as I did, and it was a lot of fun. Being out on the open road helped to clear my mind and get things into perspective. I had my bike, was back at the gym, and Sandra and I were getting on. Things couldn't be better!

While at the gym, I noticed a guy outside hanging around my bike; feeling a little nervous, I went to investigate. Once outside, I took one look at this guy and thought, wow! He resembled a Viking; he had a long blond ponytail and was humongous! So I asked him, "Like the bike do you?" He replied enthusiastically, "Oh yeah, it's gorgeous, is it yours?" Paying him a compliment, I answered, "Well, I'd trade it in to be as big as you." He just laughed, and we both headed back inside.

The next day at the gym, I was working out and saw him again, this time with his training partner; he was a lot shorter but just as muscular. I didn't want to interrupt them, so I said nothing and got on with my workout. I was in the middle of training, when I noticed him waving his arm in my direction, assuming he was trying to get someone's attention, I ignored him.

He continued waving his arm, until he finally got my attention. I decided to go over and see what he wanted. In his broad Scandinavian accent, he said, "What's the matter, can't you F***ing say hello?" Not knowing what to make of the situation, I just smiled and said, "Oh ok, hello," he then started to laugh. That was the beginning of our friendship. His name was Klaus, and he was from Denmark. I was a little star-struck; I'd never been around someone so big and popular, who wanted to be around me too.

Klaus invited me round to his place, and it was very well turned out and stylish. His flat was like a walk-in health food store; he had bulk buy sports supplements and health food bars everywhere. He also had a lovely-looking girlfriend, who was very polite. It was a golden opportunity to pick his brains and get some tips, so I bombarded him with questions.

Some time had passed, and they were now preparing for dinner, so I politely grabbed my jacket to make my exit. Klaus noticed and quickly asked, "Where are you going?" So I answered sheepishly, "Well, it's about that time, and I should be going." He had a confused look on his face, "Don't be so f***ing English and sit down; you are having dinner with us." Stunned and a little shocked at his brashness, I wasn't about to turn him down. We continued our conversation over dinner, and we got to know a lot more about each other.

"It was time to go home"

The next day at the gym, he introduced me to his training partner Phil. It looked like I was about to become the third member of the crew, and that suited me just fine. After a few weeks of training with them, I made significant improvements; but that left me wanting more. Some dynamite pills were floating around from Russia; apparently a lot better than the 50mg ones I had previously taken.

These were 200mg per tab and unknown. I was asked if I'd like to try them out, as a kind of experiment. And if I agreed, they would be free. So, in for a penny in for a pound, I went for it. If Sandra ever found out she'd hit the roof, so I kept this one quiet. Being cautious and not wanting to lose my head, just the one pill a day would be enough for me. But within weeks, the results were crazy; in such a short period of time, I had put on nearly a stone in weight, and my muscle mass had increased immeasurably.

I introduced Klaus to Sandra, but when the boys met him, they were mesmerized; he was like a real-life WWE wrestler. The boys had loads of fun with Klaus, who you could see under the scary exterior, was a good guy, unusual for types like him. He helped me out big time with two situations, Aaron needed to get his injections done, and Dean had to get his eyes tested. Sandra and I were at work, so I asked Klaus, and he happily obliged.

When he turned up at the school, the kids went crazy, and it made my boys feel special. Sandra called ahead to let the school know Klaus was coming; he was so easy to describe. Killing two birds with one stone, he decided to take them both out together. He took Aaron to get his injections first, then Dean on to his eye test, finishing up at McDonald's for lunch. He eventually got them back to school, and the boys really enjoyed their time out with him.

Klaus was getting ready for a bodybuilding contest that was coming up and was dieting hard. He needed mental space to do that, so I gave him that room. Sandra and I were getting on great, and after some thought, we decided a family break was on the cards. Finding cheap flights, we booked tickets to see my mum and Lino in Italy. Sandra and the boys were ecstatic! My old mate Darren kindly dropped us off at the airport, and we were all excited.

Arriving in Italy, the boys couldn't contain themselves; even I was thrilled for them. Sandra and the boys were blown away by the size of the mountains, and the amazing landscape. The boys' faces were glued to the car window, as they stared out at the scenery. The area around mums house was all countryside, and it had plenty of space to run around and play. Aaron and Dean took full advantage of that, and put the open space to good use.

Sandra and I got to spend some quality time together, which was well needed. We had never done anything like this as a family, and it was precious to us. Lino showed us around the mountains, and fussed over the boys; they loved the attention. One of the best moments was seeing my best friend Gerardo; I hadn't seen him in years, and he was now living with his girlfriend and their baby son Thomas. Sandra and I managed to get some alone time thanks to mum. She looked after the boys so we could go out for the evening with Gerardo and his girlfriend.

We went into the town of Turin and found it so romantic. We ate at a fancy restaurant, and then stayed for coffee. Sandra loved it. The boys enjoyed themselves so much, and we enjoyed watching them play. Unfortunately, the time had flown by so fast, that it was now time to go home. The plane got grounded because of fog, so we had to stay at the airport until the next day.

I made a quick call. "Darren its Martin, we're still in Italy, and our flights have been delayed. Would you mind picking us up at the airport in the morning? Sandra and the boys are just too shattered for the train ride home." After some mumbling, Darren replied, "Man, I've got to be up early in the morning, I tell you what, I know a good cab company, here's their"... I hung up!

"Frustrated with life and myself"

Overhearing my conversation, Sandra said, "Can't you ring Klaus and ask him?" Giving it some thought, I said, "No way! He is dieting for his competition and is hardly eating; he'll already be grumpy, not to mention ringing him at this time of the morning." It was nearly 6am. In the end, we had no choice, and I decided to take a chance. Our flight was leaving at 6.45am, so I bit the bullet.

I rang him and he answered. "Hello Klaus," there was nothing, then, "Who is it? What do you want at this time of the morning?" He sounded shattered! But I continued, "Klaus it's Martin, I don't suppose"... He interjected. "Martin, are you asking for a lift?" Not wanting to waste his time any longer, I said, "Yes please, we're coming into Stansted airport, and our flight gets in at 9:50am. So if"... He interjected again, "See you there." And click; he put the phone down. No sooner had I finished that conversation, an announcement came over the tannoy.

Our plane would now be leaving even later, and we would arrive around 12.30pm; that was just our luck! There was no way I was going to ring Klaus again, not after that last conversation. We conceded he'd be furious with us, and we'd have to make our own way home. Our flight finally left, and we got back into Stansted airport at nearly 1pm. We checked out and headed towards the exit gate, and would you believe it, Klaus was waiting for us. He checked the flight times and saw the delays, and he still showed up, what a legend! We finally got home and unpacked our bags, but I was hiding something. While in Italy, no one covered for me at work, so now back home, my boss wanted to know where I had been.

Explaining my family situation to him, he was relatively sympathetic, but still wasn't happy with me. We agreed that maybe it was in everyone's best interest if we went our separate ways, and that was the end of my employment. I needed to figure out what to do with my life.

It wasn't long before we were in financial trouble again, and there was nothing we could do to fix it. After much thought and conversation, I sold my bike to pay off some of the finance on it, and Sandra agreed to take out a 10k loan to pay off the rest, and leave some spare to buy a car for her.

The bike was finally gone, and it was time to purchase a car for Sandra. Klaus and I went to check out a Vauxhall Corsa in Welwyn Garden City, that Sandra had identified. We haggled with the lady and got it for a reasonable price. Sandra loved it, and she was happy getting around independently.

Several weeks had gone by, and I was hitting the gym really hard, and I was juiced up pretty good too. Our lives were slowly drifting apart, and as that happened, I felt this family would be better off without me. I was like dead weight. Nothing made me happy; I was frustrated with life and myself, regularly yelling at the kids and getting into blazing rows with Sandra. Something had to give.

CHAPTER 10

UNBLEMISHED LOVE

Opportunities were limited, but I had one presented to me. Klaus was moving back to Denmark, and invited me to join him. Seeing as I had left a trail of mess behind me, it wasn't a difficult decision to make. I couldn't do anything right for this family, and felt like a constant disappointment. I spoke to Sandra about it, and she didn't seem too bothered, she was probably relieved.

So one evening while pondering it for hours, I eventually decided to pick up the phone and booked my ticket. Putting the phone down, I turned to Sandra and said, "It's done, I'm gone." She broke down in tears, and it ripped my heart out. Klaus was busy packing his stuff at the flat, while getting it ready for shipment, so I didn't see him at the gym. I began training with Phil for a while, and he was very level headed.

"Jesus loves you!"

While training, Phil spoke to me about my situation. He mentioned my move to Denmark, and leaving my family behind, he didn't think it was a good idea and tried to talk me out of it. My experimentation with steroids wasn't helping me at all, and it was now destroying me physically as well as mentally. I was experiencing terrible pain in my kidneys, and Phil was worried for me.

The thing I most liked about him was this; he had nothing to lose by giving me bad advice, but chose to point me in the right direction. Phil helped me manage my usage, and told me I could use half the amount I did. As I was pretty strong, he assured me I could do a lot better without it. Interestingly enough, it wasn't long after that conversation that I became severely ill, and was unable to travel to Denmark. While recuperating, Phil helped me out by giving me a job as his driver. I drove him to different locations around England,

and he paid me very generously, Sometimes £100 for a day's work. However, the trips were very few and far between. He was making incredible amounts of money, and promised to set me up with some work in the New Year. He decided to go back home for Christmas, and would see me when he got back. Klaus was arrested in Denmark, and was sent to prison. That's when we lost contact.

Christmas was coming, and I was out of work. Unable to pay off the £245 a month loan, not including our utility bills and other family stuff, we were in trouble. And if I thought things couldn't get any worse, I was wrong. Mum called to say that Lino had just finished with her, and told her never to come back. I called him to find out what was going on; and he said he couldn't take the abuse any longer. He didn't want to see her again, and just like that! Mums life in Italy was now over.

Not only was mum exiled from Italy, it meant I was too. There were no more escape routes for me, and I convinced myself I'd be ok, but not this time. The fuel that regularly got me over the line had finally run out, and my life felt like quicksand. I had never come across this sense of helplessness before, and I was scared, which then manifested as anger. With all the money worries that surrounded us, as well as the Christmas holidays, Sandra and I got into a massive argument; this was our worse row ever.

We got so heated, that it actually turned physical. While shouting at each other, Sandra got up in my face, and I pushed her away. She then tripped over the step, and fell backwards onto the living room floor. She got into a flying temper and charged at me, and that's all I remember. When I came to, Sandra was cowering on the floor as I kicked her. My youngest son was racked with fear, while looking up at me yelling, "Alright Dad, alright!" I just froze.

Sandra quickly got up to her feet, but I didn't wait to hear what she was going to say. I already knew the script. I had been here so many times now... it was time for me to leave. With nowhere else to go, I ended up back at mums. She was finally alone, and now I was too. Moving back into that house was soul destroying, as it held some of the worst memories ever. And now at the age of thirty-three, my life had ended up right back were it started. I missed Sandra, but being away from my kids was the toughest obstacle I had ever come across. I smiled while out with friends, and tried to keep a lid on my feelings, but deep down inside I was dying. It was made worse by more bloody Christians asking to pray with me on the street. They kept telling me Jesus loved me and had a plan for my life. A plan for my life? Are you f***ing kidding me?

I heard so much about that man, but it never made a difference. Yes, at times I will admit, it did make me feel better, but I always ended up back in a hole, so what use was that! A friend told me about him, Angie's mum was a good friend of His, and I even heard a sick person crying out to him from a hospital bed. But it did nothing for me. So I just couldn't be bothered with it.

I distinctly remember that day, when my friend Mark and I walking through a busy market which was bustling with people. A lady screamed at the top of her voice, "Hey you!" Everyone turned to look, and with her pointed finger aimed right at me, she roared, "Jesus loves you!" Feeling a little embarrassed, I yelled back, "Yeah, I love him too," as we walked away. I never told Mark, but even though our conversation continued, her words stuck with me.

I occasionally called Sandra, but my pride got in the way, and caused more arguments. My mind was plagued by my past failures, and was working overtime. Whenever I tried to lie down and relax, thoughts would play out in my mind like a movie, over and over. Starting from the beginning, they showed me all the damage I had caused, and the destruction that always followed me. Trying to sleep was useless and going to the gym lost its lustre. Nothing motivated me!

"Ending my life"

Sinking deeper into depression, the hospital was my only refuge. I turned up there late one night, and asked them to section me; it was for my own protection. I got to a point where I didn't feel safe being on my own. They refused me on the grounds of cognisance; but I wasn't there because I was crazy, just extremely vulnerable. Feeling so depressed and with nowhere to turn, it seemed there was only one way out, suicide. Courage was never my strong point, although many thought it was. I achieved my rep by doing the things I did, but it doesn't take a hero to do stupid stuff.

You just need to be angry, confused and anxious enough, and that'll make you do crazy things. For the first time in my life, work eluded me; there were no prospects, no purpose and no direction; it felt like the walls were closing in on me. It was suffocating! All my bridges were burnt, there was no way back to the other side; I was alone.

It was early evening, and I needed to free my mind, so I got out of the house and wandered the streets aimlessly. I found myself standing outside Carol's old flat from years earlier, reminiscing on the past and all the crazy stuff that went on. When I turned around and looked across the road, I saw the church opposite, and the lights were on. I never noticed that church before, yet it was always there, how strange. So many people told me about Jesus, and the benefits of going to church, but I just couldn't get my head around it. Well, I had no other choice now but to find out for myself.

It took me a while to pluck up the courage to go inside, but I had nothing to lose. Walking through the doors, I found myself a seat at the very back of the building, desperately trying to go unnoticed; it was fairly packed, so I sat down and fixed my eyes on the preacher. He was an American named Dennis DeGrasse; and he had a funny sense of humour. I don't remember much about the sermon, because my mind was revolving like a cyclone. I just needed to know everything was going to be ok.

The preacher then picked random people out in the congregation, and started telling them what God was saying to him about them; he shared some deep personal stuff too. That got my attention! I knew I needed a word, I honestly did! Then I had an internal argument, you don't even believe in God, why are you here? Look at yourself.

But the truth is, I couldn't trust myself anymore. I needed to get rid of that horrible lost sinking feeling inside me, which was crying out for something... Anything! After speaking to many people, and bringing most of them to tears, the preacher then stopped; my heart sank. Staring at the old parquet floor, I contemplated my next move, and there was only one option.... ending my life. There was no word for me, of course there wasn't, there never would be. What was I thinking coming in here? I was completely defeated. Suddenly, a voice came over the speakers, "If anyone would like prayer, please come over, and I will be happy to pray with you." It was the preacher again; he's not finished. That's when my desperation turned to shame. I was eager to go up, but had never done anything like this in public before; I wondered what the established Christians would think? But after having a word with myself, I self-consciously walked towards the preacher, and stood patiently waiting my turn.

"Go home, your comfort is there"

By now he was already praying for a lot of people, and there was a small queue. So I took the time to ask myself, who can I ask him to pray for? Maybe I'll get him to pray for my sister, that'll work. It was my turn, so I sat down. He looked at me with a big smile on his face, "What would you like me to pray for?" With my pre-prepared speech, I said, "Can you please pray for my sister, she is addicted to heroin and crack cocaine, and needs help." He prayed for Susan, and his prayers were very striking and sincere, that it gave me a warm feeling in my stomach.

When he finished, I got up, shook his hand politely and said thank you. But when I turned to leave, he grabbed me by the arm, and sat me back in my chair. No man had handled me before, so I admired his nerve. He got my attention by looking me directly in the eyes, "What about you?" Those three words gripped me! I just froze; I suddenly wanted to run and get away, but deep down inside, I knew there was no way out.

So conceding, I finally mustered the strength to answer. I never wanted to be in this position, because I knew it would make me vulnerable. But it was too late. My chin started to quiver, and he had breached my barriers, the words finally came. "I just feel lost." finally, I was able to cry.

I held that in for so many years, and it all came out in one hit. As he prayed for me, whipping up a storm and crying out to God, I was completely and utterly broken. I had never been so vulnerable in my life, and it was liberating! He was holding me while praying with no restrictions, no questions, no hesitations, just complete acceptance. By this time, I was crying uncontrollably, as his prayers echoed in the distance.

That's when it happened! As he prayed, I felt a warm sensation at the very tip of my toes, and then it started to travel up my legs, and continued up my body. He was still praying, and I was still crying, but I was aware it was happening, and kept perfectly still. It felt like being filled with hot water or lava, and as it got higher, it got stronger until it reached my head. That's when the pressure became immense, and then it suddenly lifted.

It felt like the entire weight of the world had been lifted off my shoulders, and replaced with a full manifestation of Gods love and mercy. I was still crying and stood up to thank him from the bottom of my heart, but as I shook his hand and glanced around the church; something was different.

Everything looked like it was in high definition, and even the sound was sharper. It was as if I had been looking at life through a clouded window. So, turning to walk away, another man approached me and asked if he could pray for me too. I couldn't believe my luck. It was incredible. He then led me through something called the Sinner's Prayer, and it was significant to my life - I definitely needed it.

Leaving the church, I couldn't wait to visit some Christian friend's and share what happened; surely they'd be excited. On arrival I was unable to stay seated, but paced up and down while smiling uncontrollably. But they had become a little concerned, and told me to calm down and take things slow.

Feeling suppressed, and not wanting to be rude, I left. My intention was to go home, but as I walked down the path and grabbed the gate, a voice startled me. It repeated the same words, "Go home, your comfort is there. Go home, your comfort is there." it was as clear as crystal. It wasn't an audible voice, but came from inside me.

Engulfed by real peace, I knew it was finally time for me to go home, my real home. To Sandra and the kids. It was getting pretty late, but for some reason, I knew it would be ok. Reaching the door of the house, I noticed the living room light was on; so I knocked softly. I heard someone coming.... my oldest son Aaron answered - "Dad!" He shouted, grabbing me around my waist and hugging me tightly.

I walked him into the hallway, and closed the front door behind us both. Still holding onto Aaron, I reached the entrance of the living room. Sandra was sitting on the floor reading a book to my youngest son Dean. As I tried to step across the threshold, it happened again... I broke down in tears. Aaron looked up at me and asked inquisitively, "Dad, why are you crying?" Trying to catch my breath, I answered, "I've just never been this happy!" In ten years, Sandra had never seen me shed a single tear! She cried as she rushed to her feet to hug me, and the boys joined in; we all cried while hugging each other. I moved back in that night, and everything changed.

"You won't be seeing me again"

I was under constant scrutiny for the rest of that week, and Sandra was still coming to terms with what just happened to me. As the days went on, Sandra became more and more curious about what exactly happened, and I could see her trying to work out where the REAL Martin was. What she hadn't realised was this; the old me was dead! It was an entirely different person sitting in front of her.

She pestered me for ages about coming to that church, and I got jealous about sharing my newfound faith, and tried to put her off. The following Sunday, we attended the church as a family, and the boys loved it, Sandra didn't say too much, but I could see it had an impact on her. We attended again the following week, and during the worship service, Sandra burst into tears. The pastor and his wife came over to pray with her; I stood in awe, wondering if the same thing was happening to her.

When we got home, she opened up. She shared her heart with me, "I've been going to church my whole life, but always had this niggling feeling deep down inside, that somehow, there had to be more than this, there just had to be. There were times when I wanted to scream in frustration. A relationship with Jesus was all I ever longed for... and it's finally happened!"

As she spoke, the transformation in her face was evident; her eyes lit up, and she became so animated and excited while sharing it with me. We were instantly adopted into our new church family, and did whatever we could to serve. Our lives were so different now and changed so much in such a short period too.

We attended an Alpha course, joined a lifegroup, and never missed a Sunday service. I wanted to be baptised, so I asked pastor Brendan to come round with his wife to give us a talk on it. He came round later that week and taught us all about it. While we were speaking, I shared about what God had been doing in our lives, and after a few minutes, Brendan slammed his book shut saying, "You've just given me every reason why you should be baptised." He continued to encourage us throughout the evening.

The following Sunday, announcements were given on the upcoming baptisms. "Just to let everyone know, next week Martin and Sandra will be getting baptised." The announcements hadn't finished when Sandra looked at me and said, "No one told me I was getting baptised next Sunday!" Grinning back at her, I whispered, "Well, you are now!" She just smiled.

Sunday came around quickly, and there we were, waiting to go into the waters of baptism. Listening to Sandra giving a short testimony choked me a little, but watching her baptism brought me to tears. It was now my turn. Sid, the church doorman for the last forty years, was holding my towel while waiting for me to come back out. But, as I stepped into the water, it dawned on me. So pausing and turning back to him, I reached out my hand and said, "I'll say goodbye now Sid, you won't be seeing me again."

Sid pulled me into his chest and cried his heart out – and I did too. Finally getting back into the water, Brendan earnestly prayed over my life as I stood there whimpering like a little-lost kid. Then the realisation of the death and resurrection of Jesus Christ, and it's life changing power overwhelmed me; that's when I knew for sure, the old me wasn't coming back up.

Two months after our baptisms, Sandra and I decided to make an announcement at our lifegroup. We were finally getting married. It stirred up such excitement, that even the congregation rallied to do their part for it. It was incredible.

We found out pastor Brendan could marry us at the church, so we made arrangements and set the date. We told our families and got everything put in place. Pastor Brendan married us, and apart from our immediate family, the church congregation were our guests.

Being a multicultural church meant the food was going to be diverse and very tasty.

It was prepared for our special day. God was good to us; between the church and a few friends, we had a traditional white wedding, a car, photographers, the reception, and free catering too.

The Gospel Centre invested in our new lives, and we were truly honoured and humbled, but most importantly... reconciled to God and each other.

THIS STORY CONTINUES

In the sequel to this book, "NOT CRAZY, JUST CALLED."

As time went on, God led me through many manifestations in the rescuing of countless lost souls, which launched me into international apostolic ministry and eventually led me to plant churches and initiate new ministries.

It's the continuation of the incredible journey God has and still is taking me on. Along with my wife and two sons.

FINAL THOUGHTS

In all my life I never envisioned such a dramatic transformation taking place the way it did that cold November evening. When God called me to write this book many years ago, that too was an incredible miracle, especially coming from an unschooled background like mine. That in itself speaks of the incredible life-changing power of Christ, and Gods plan and purpose for us all.

If you have taken time to read this book, my prayer is this...

That God would reveal His love to you through His son Jesus Christ, and that He would impart to you a full manifestation of His love and presence in your life.

May this book bless you and enrich your life by the truth of its contents. Amen.

- Martin Berry

ᴕMETHING TO CONSIDER

If you have read this book, and are not a Christian or just haven't ever contemplated giving your life to Jesus, I would like to invite you to consider praying this prayer. It is my wish that you might experience the life changing power of Christ. This is a simple but powerful prayer, and must not be taken lightly.

If you pray this prayer and believe it in your heart, I truly believe that Jesus will answer you...

"Dear Lord Jesus, I am sorry for all the things I have done wrong.

I ask for your forgiveness, and I now turn away from everything that I know is wrong and I ask for your help to change me.

Fill me with your Holy Spirit and equip me with everything that I need to start my new life with you.

Thank you for paying for me with your blood on the Cross.

I now receive your gift of salvation.

Be the lord of my life, now and forever.

In Jesus name Amen."

May the Lord bless you and increase you in every area of your life.

- Martin Berry